PIZZAZZERIE

PIZZAZZERIE
Entertain in Style

Courtney Dial Whitmore

with Phronsie Dial

Photography by Evin Krehbiel

Foreword by Tori Spelling

GIBBS SMITH
TO ENRICH AND INSPIRE HUMANKIND

First Edition

21 20 19 18 17   5 4 3 2 1

Published by

Gibbs Smith

P.O. Box 667

Layton, Utah 84041

1.800.835.4993 orders

www.gibbs-smith.com

Designed by Tracy Sunrize Johnson

Printed and bound in China

Gibbs Smith books are printed on either recycled, 100% post-consumer waste, FSC-certified papers or on paper produced from sustainable PEFC-certified forest/controlled wood source. Learn more at www.pefc.org.

Library of Congress Cataloging-in-Publication Data

Names: Whitmore, Courtney Dial, author.

Title: Pizzazzerie : entertain in style / Courtney Dial Whitmore with Phronsie Dial ; photography by Evin Krehbiel ; foreword by Tori Spelling.

Description: First edition. | Layton, Utah : Gibbs Smith, [2017]

Identifiers: LCCN 2017000283 | ISBN 9781423645528 (hardcover)

Subjects: LCSH: Entertaining. | Cooking. | Parties. | Menus.

Classification: LCC TX731 .W474 2017 | DDC 642/.4—dc23

LC record available at https://lccn.loc.gov/2017000283

For my darling hostess-in-training, Blakely:

Start each day like it's your birthday,
and leave a little confetti everywhere you go!

CONTENTS

FOREWORD

BY TORI SPELLING

P arties have always been in my blood. If you have *Pizzazzerie: Entertain in Style* in hand, you're likely a party-lover yourself. As a young girl, I watched my mother throw the most beautiful parties. They were exquisitely executed, and her attention to detail was meticulous. I learned from the best. As an adult, my parties aren't anywhere on the scale of my mother's, but what I did learn was that it's all about the details. That's the difference between a good party and a great party.

These little details, the ones that put your own personal touch into each party, are my favorite part of entertaining. I believe anything we create comes directly from the heart—*homemade* equals *love*, and I have raised my kids to believe in that as well. It's a great party planning motto! My kids have watched me DIY, craft, and party plan since they were born—I've created little party monsters! My kids plan my parties with me from conception to execution, especially their own birthday parties. I always ask them to start with a theme or a vision for the party, and then we move on to color palette. They love the process as much as I do. If you have children or grandchildren, get them involved in the entire party process like Courtney and I do with our own little ones. Wonderful party memories can be made as much in the planning of an event as in the execution.

So what are you waiting for? You're about to discover dozens of creative ideas, and clever ways to personalize them, throughout these pages. No matter the time of year, your guest list, or your budget, Courtney has provided you with all the tools you need. Remember, the overall look and feel of your party is important, but it's those personal details that your guests will remember. Happy party planning!

Love
Tori

INTRODUCTION

"That's what life is all about: Let's have a party. Let's have it tonight."
—Lilly Pulitzer

Entertaining, in its simplest form, is the art of creating memories: birthdays, holidays, dinner parties . . . With this book, you'll be inspired to set the stage for beautiful gatherings all year long, from a New Year's Day Brunch (page 21) to A Christmas Dinner (page 181), and every occasion in between.

My mother is the ultimate hostess. Growing up in the South, I learned quite a bit about monogramming linens and polishing silver from her. Every afternoon when I came home from school, I found my mother designing tablescapes in our formal dining room. On long road trips, she would organize her favorite magazine clippings in a three-ring binder so she would *never* forget a fabulous idea. In other words, she created her own form of Pinterest back in the '80s!—from handmade gingerbread house favors to bite-sized appetizers as far as the eye could see. While she and I each have our own distinct style, her influence on my life is crystal clear.

My love affair with the art of entertaining began when I was a single twenty-something in my first "real" job after graduate school. I finally had a dining room all my own and was able to host dinner parties, Halloween parties, Christmas parties, and more in that small Nashville townhouse. It was after my very first party (a black-and-white themed birthday party for a friend) that I created Pizzazzerie.com, and I have been sharing entertaining inspiration ever since! I'm fairly certain that at that first party the food was cold, the place settings were all wrong, and I probably broke every hostess "rule" in the book—but I don't remember any of those things. I remember smiling, laughing, and spending time with people dear to me. This, my friends, is the reason to entertain!

So kick off your heels, grab a glass of champagne, and be inspired to create your own celebrations all year long. It is my sincere hope that you discover new traditions for yourself and your loved ones within these pages. Consider the table your canvas and paint away! Your art will become the setting for lifelong memories of toasts, laughs, hugs, and togetherness.

XO,
Courtney

HOW TO USE THIS BOOK

**WELCOME TO YOUR VERY OWN ENTERTAINING GUIDE!
IF YOU DON'T HAVE A CATERER OR FLORIST ON SPEED DIAL,
THEN YOU'RE IN THE RIGHT PLACE.**

Here you'll find more than a dozen celebrations with easy-to-follow instructions in every chapter: recipes, tips and tricks, DIY ideas, and photos. Many of the projects are simple and can be done ahead of time so you can actually enjoy your party.

If you are a novice entertainer, you'll find "user-friendly" ideas, recipes, and table settings. If you are a seasoned entertainer, you'll discover new and unique touches to enhance your table settings all year long.

Mix and match not only the recipes but also the DIYs, color schemes, and more; you now have everything you need to create a stylish celebration that's totally "you." Be sure to reference the Mix It Up section (page 196) for additional party ideas.

There are no rules, except to have fun. I hope to ease the stress of entertaining and get back to the true spirit of the occasion. Remember, don't get caught up in making everything perfect. Focus on great food, drinks, and setting a festive environment; the guests will do the rest!

ENTERTAINING BASICS

**WHETHER YOU'RE HOSTING FOUR PEOPLE OR FIFTY,
HERE ARE A FEW ENTERTAINING BASICS TO KEEP IN MIND.**

Are there rules for creating a guest list?

Keep your guest list interesting by inviting a variety of people from young to old. Your friends will enjoy meeting new people, so mix it up! For dinner parties, keep the total between six and ten guests so you can be seated comfortably (couples don't always have to be seated together). Game nights or viewing parties work best with less than a dozen guests, while mix-and-mingle style cocktail parties allow for several dozen or more depending on the size of your space. As a rule of thumb, you will usually have a third of invitees unable to attend, so plan accordingly.

When do I send out invitations? Are email invitations appropriate?

For special celebrations, always send paper invitations at least four weeks in advance. Casual gatherings allow for online invitations, though they should still be sent several weeks in advance. Remember to always include what the event is, the date and time, location, who is hosting the party, and RSVP details.

If you really want to wow your guests, consider hand-delivery or mailing a little package with party elements along with the invitation (party horn, party hat, mask, etc. Just don't send confetti or glitter. As festive as it may seem, no one will appreciate picking up the debris).

How do I care for linens?

Wash linens with like colors. Steam iron with a little starch for a crisp look to your tablecloth and napkins.

 TIP: *For one-of-a-kind tablecloths, buy a few yards of fabric in a color and design that complement your dishes and decorations. It's so easy that you won't even need a sewing machine, just a needle and thread or no-sew hem tape.*

Where do I put all the items on the table?

Don't fret if you've never officially set a fancy tablescape. Reference this illustration whenever you need a place setting reminder.

How should I prep ahead for my party?

Enjoy the party yourself by setting the table in advance—sometimes as early as the night before. Be sure you're dressed and everything is nearly complete (except for pulling out hot foods and filling ice) one hour before the party. This will give you a moment to relax, especially because at least one guest will inevitably show up early.

Choose food that can be prepared in advance, and keep the rest simple and easy to pull together. Open filled bottles so guests feel comfortable helping themselves. For seated affairs, always have pitchers and carafes of extra drinks so you can easily refill guests' beverages. Be sure one glass at each place setting is devoted to water.

What items should I keep stocked in my kitchen?

Always have a few "basics" on hand for last-minute parties, including white dinnerware, basic serving platters, and unscented candles. Keep your pantry stocked with mixed nuts, crackers, and fine chocolate for quick serving. Always have a sparkling water, champagne, and white wine chilled and ready to serve.

What items should I keep stocked in my bar?

Keep a well-stocked bar either displayed on a bar cart or tucked away in a sideboard or kitchen. I recommend stocking gin, vodka, Scotch, whiskey, rum, and tequila. Be sure to have mixers and enhancers like lime juice, tomato juice, club soda, tonic water, and soda. It's also always a good idea to have white wine, red wine, and one sparkling variety on hand. Keep your alcohol "party ready" by tucking away cute cocktail napkins and drink stirrers with your collection.

Are there any tips for party layout?

Be sure your guests don't get stuck in a long line for a drink or spend half the party wandering in search of a trash can. For mix-and-mingle parties, remove the chairs to your dining table to allow for easy flow around the room. Greet your guests and quickly let them know where drinks are being served. Tuck a trash can under the table or beside a buffet server. Be sure all items are easy to reach and accessible.

How do I keep the food and drinks topped off and still enjoy the party?

Keep extra food warmed in the oven or chilled in the refrigerator. If you see a tray getting low, quickly fill it up and get back to the party! For larger parties, consider delegating roles to a close friend or family member. Keeping the trays filled was always my role at my mother's parties!

Do you have any music recommendations?

One of the best ways to set a festive mood at a party is through music. If you don't have wired speakers in your home, use a Bluetooth speaker and select a music station with a variety that is fitting for your party. Be sure it's not too loud for guests to talk.

How do I greet guests and make them feel welcome?

Be near the door to greet your guests as they arrive. If they have a coat, offer to take it for them and let them know you'll be placing it in a coat closet or a tucked-away room, like a guest bedroom. Serve them a cocktail, or direct them to the bar. Lastly, if they look lost, be sure to introduce them to other guests they may have previously met or have something in common with, which you should mention during the introduction: "This is my friend Kelley. She just got back from a fabulous trip to Scotland!" You want your guests to feel as comfortable as possible. Relax. If you're having a wonderful time, your guests will too.

Don't fret if something doesn't go as planned; it's bound to happen.

How do I tell my guests the party is over?

To signify the end of the party, slowly begin bringing plates and serving platters into the kitchen. I never let my guests help with clean up; they're quickly told, "Absolutely not!" Graciously let your guests know that you were thrilled they could come, and you look forward to celebrating together again soon.

What's the easiest way to clean up, and what items do I keep?

Store plastic bags and freezer containers in quick reach for easy pack up and storage of extra food. Quickly begin a dishwashing load so you'll have less to do on the morning after the party. Be sure to save any items you can reuse, such as silk flowers, extra cocktail napkins, or candles. Consider keeping a place card, invitation, or banner as a memento of the party.

What do I do if . . .

. . . someone spills wine? Keep a few "go-to" cleaning items tucked away in your kitchen. For spilled wine, blot the area with club soda and use Wine Away (available at retail stores) on the spot. For larger red wine spills on the carpet or furniture, sprinkle table salt liberally on the stain and follow with rug cleaner. Use a wet towel and a dab of dish soap to remove general food stains.

. . . someone gets hurt? Also keep a small first aid kit (pain reliever included) on hand for any small injuries that might occur, especially if children are present.

. . . a guest had a little too much to drink? Always offer to call a cab for any party guest that has consumed too much alcohol. Consider having water bottles on hand to give out if needed.

. . . I didn't know my guest was a vegetarian? Be flexible for last-minute changes such as guests with dietary restrictions. Be sure to serve a variety of foods and always have non-alcoholic options on hand. For seated dinner parties, consider asking guests to include any dietary restrictions in their RSVP so you can plan accordingly.

New Year's Day Brunch

KICK OFF THE NEW YEAR WITH GLITZ AND GLAMOUR!

Since most calendars are booked with New Year's Eve events, shake things up by welcoming the new year with the best meal of all— brunch. Set up a glittery New Year's Day Brunch full of sweet and savory favorites, mini boxes of confetti, and a rosé mimosa bar. Don't worry, these recipes can *all* be prepped ahead of time and popped into the oven the morning of your gathering.

 TIP: *If you're planning on painting the town red on New Year's Eve, I suggest prepping the tablescape ahead of time.*

Pick up simple glass vases to double as favors for guests as well as centerpieces for the table. Fill them with a variety of flowers and a place card tucked down among the blooms. Guests will adore taking home their pretty vase.

Confetti in mini clear boxes gives each guest a handful of their own to toss in celebration.

 TIP: *A glittered fabric table covering provides the ultimate ambiance of shimmer and sparkle.*

In addition to the flower vases, your rosé bottles will add pops of pink down the table (and allow quick access for refills).

Another party embellishment which can be applied to any type of celebration, is printed menus, signs, gift tags—you name it! I created these simple *Happy New Year* plate toppers on my computer, printed them on a sturdy card stock, and placed them in the center of each plate for an extra welcoming effect on the tablescape.

Eat

Serve all your brunch favorites, but give them a dainty touch, such as mini stacked pancakes finished with a ribbon skewer, coffee cake on an heirloom cake stand, and fruit in mini gold cupcake liners for easy serving.

Florentine Tartlets

1 cup Bisquick

1²/₃ cups milk

1¹/₂ cups grated Monterey Jack cheese

1¹/₂ cups grated cheddar cheese

5 eggs, beaten

¹/₂ cup chopped onion

1 cup shredded carrots

1 cup finely chopped ham

1 (10-ounce) package frozen chopped spinach, cooked and drained well (use paper towels to pat out all of the moisture)

1 garlic clove, minced

¹/₂ teaspoon salt

Preheat oven to 375° F. Mix all ingredients until well blended. Spray miniature or regular-sized muffin tins with nonstick cooking spray, and fill each ²/₃ full with batter. Bake for 20–25 minutes for regular muffins and 18–20 minutes for miniature. Prepare in advance, keeping the muffin batter in the refrigerator for up to 2 days. Bake the morning of the party.

YIELD: 48 MINIATURE TARTLETS OR 24 REGULAR MUFFIN TARTLETS

Overnight Coffee Cake

¾ cup butter, softened

1 cup sugar

1 cup sour cream

2 eggs

2 cups all-purpose flour

1 teaspoon nutmeg

½ teaspoon salt

1 teaspoon baking soda

¾ cup packed light brown sugar

¾ cup chopped pecans

2 teaspoons cinnamon

Combine the butter, sugar, and sour cream and beat until fluffy. Add the eggs and mix well. Next, add the flour, nutmeg, salt, and baking soda to the batter and stir until well blended. Pour into a greased 9 x 13-inch pan or divide between two 8-inch cake pans. Combine the brown sugar, pecans, and cinnamon and sprinkle over the batter. Cover and chill overnight. When ready to bake, preheat over to 350° F, uncover and bake for 35–40 minutes.

YIELD: 12 SERVINGS

Coffee Cake Glaze

1 cup powdered sugar

1 tablespoon milk

½ teaspoon vanilla extract

Combine all the ingredients and beat until smooth. Drizzle over the cake while it is still warm.

Drink

Roll out a bar cart for the ultimate rosé mimosa bar, and encourage guests to build their perfect mimosa. Set out all the mix-ins, like a variety of juices and, of course, lots of rosé! I suggest pouring juices out of their store-bought containers and into simple glass carafes to keep the presentation chic and simple. Consider adding a dish of berries or other garnishes to the bar cart for festive drink embellishments.

More drink station ideas: Bloody Mary bar, hot cocoa bar, coffee or tea station, fruit-infused water bar, or a mint julep bar (page 44).

Rosé Mimosa

¾ cup chilled sparkling rosé

¼ cup fruit juice (orange, grapefruit, etc.)

Pour sparkling rosé into a champagne flute. Top with your favorite fruit juice. Cheers!

YIELD: 1 MIMOSA

 TIP: *Don't fret if you don't have a bar cart. A console table or coffee table can be set up in a similar fashion.*

Create

Let the gilded touches continue with one of my favorite DIY elements, painted charger plates! I started creating these larger decorative plates several years ago when I had trouble finding the perfect match for a party. I fell in love with creating dozens of chargers in different hues to fashion the perfect base for my dinnerware. For these, a hint of gold foil adds a surprising touch that ties in beautifully with the gold-rimmed dinnerware and gold flatware.

DIY: Painted Gold Leaf Chargers

Dinnerware charger plates (any color will do; find at Michaels or other craft store)

Primer spray paint

Acrylic paints

Paintbrushes

Gold foil sheets

Prime your chargers with spray paint so they're ready to be painted. Then simply pick your favorite colors and use brush-strokes to create a pattern. While paint is drying, add on a touch of gold foil around the charger. Allow to fully dry. Use underneath dinner-sized plates.

 TIP: *Clear glass plates also look very chic over the chargers and allow the pattern to show through.*

Derby Party

OFF TO THE RACES!

Y ou might not find yourself in Kentucky for the races, but you can still entertain in style before *and* after the two-minute race. Did you know that the first derby was run in 1875? The races are now America's longest-running sporting event—that's worth celebrating! I've pulled a few "Kentucky must-haves" together along with some additional Southern favorites to give you a delicious Derby Party menu.

Whether you're in the infield or just watching at home with friends and neighbors, prep your party table with a bright tablecloth representative of the jockey's jerseys—like a bold green and white stripe.

 TIP: *Don't forget to visit your local fabric store for an abundance of tablecloth design options.*

For your tablescape, use a trophy-style silver bucket to hold long-stemmed roses, adding height to the table and making a big impact.

Display a horse figurine alongside your vase and scatter horseshoes for extra party décor.

 TIP: *As an alternative to cupcakes, consider creating a horseshoe-shaped cake out of a sheet cake and decorating it with chocolate frosting and piped red roses.*

For that extra wow factor, grow your own grass centerpiece. Nestle the bucket of roses down into the grass as the perfect display for prepared mint juleps. We added fence-style sides to our grass display by using miniature size picket fences from the craft store—it's amazing what you can find just wandering the craft store aisles.

Food and drink are of the utmost importance at the "Run for the Roses" so follow along for tips and tricks to help make your menu both delicious and thematic.

Eat

Serve easy-to-eat appetizers and finger foods in mini trophies found at any party store. We filled ours with a spicy ranch dip and vegetables. One of the best tips I can give for mix-and-mingle parties (especially viewing parties) is to be sure the food you're serving is simple to eat. For instance, tie in the traditional pimento cheese served at the Derby with Crispy Pimento Cheese Cups.

Candied Bourbon Pecans (page 41) are the perfect snack mix to serve in silver bowls. Or send your guests home with a bag of them tied off with a big red ribbon and a mini bottle of bourbon.

Crispy Pimento Cheese Cups

These toast cups are the first to go at every single one of my mother's parties, and people beg her for the recipe. We're finally sharing the secret! We recommend filling them with pimento cheese, but you can also fill them with chicken salad, spinach artichoke dip, or another dip-style appetizer.

Pimento Cheese Filling

- **2 cups grated sharp cheddar cheese**
- **1 (4-ounce) jar diced pimientos, do not drain**
- **1 cup mayonnaise**
- **1/8 teaspoon salt**
- **1/4 teaspoon hot pepper sauce, or 1 jalapeño pepper, finely chopped**

Combine all the ingredients until well mixed. Cover and chill for at least 2 hours.

Crispy Toast Cups

- **1 loaf thinly sliced sandwich bread**
- **1/2 cup butter, softened**

Preheat oven to 350° F. Using a rolling pin, roll each slice of bread slightly and use a 2-inch biscuit cutter or cookie cutter to cut out two rounds from each slice. Each loaf of bread has about 18 slices, not using the end slices. After cutting the bread rounds, brush the inside of the miniature muffin tins with butter, and then carefully fit the bread rounds into the muffin tins. Brush the top of the bread rounds with butter. Bake the empty cups for 10 minutes. Remove from oven and fill the cups with Pimento Cheese Filling. Bake again for 5–7 minutes. These cups are twice baked, making them very crispy and delicious.

YIELD: 36 TOAST CUPS

Beef Tenderloin Rolls

With all the bourbon tasting and mint julep drinking, you'll definitely want to serve a substantial appetizer like Beef Tenderloin Rolls. They're topped with a spicy mayonnaise and can be easily prepared the day before the party.

1 (4- to 6-pound) beef tenderloin

1 teaspoon salt

1 teaspoon garlic salt

$\frac{1}{2}$ teaspoon pepper

24 bread rolls

Preheat oven to 450° F. Rub the tenderloin with salts and pepper. Sear the meat in a hot frying pan for several minutes on each side and then transfer to a baking dish to bake for 20 minutes. Allow the meat to rest for 20–30 minutes. Slice and serve on your favorite roll with spicy mayonnaise (or your favorite spread).

YIELD: 20-24 ROLLS

TIP: *Our favorite rolls are Ukrop's white house rolls.*

Spicy Mayonnaise

1 cup mayonnaise

1 teaspoon lemon juice

1 tablespoon Dijon mustard

1 teaspoon horseradish (optional)

Combine ingredients and stir until blended. Cover and refrigerate until needed.

Candied Bourbon Pecans

These Candied Bourbon Pecans are not only simple to make but also addictively delicious. They're the perfect crunchy snack for watching the races.

1 cup firmly packed light brown sugar

¼ cup bourbon

4 tablespoons unsalted butter

½ teaspoon salt

¼ cup honey

3–4 cups raw pecan halves

Combine brown sugar, bourbon, butter, salt, and honey in a medium saucepan over medium heat. Stir until combined and melted. Add in pecans and stir to coat. Continue stirring until the liquid thickens and pecans are glazed. Spread on parchment-lined cookie sheet and allow to cool. Once cooled, break into pieces and enjoy.

YIELD: 3–4 CUPS

Chocolate Pecan Bars

I've given the classic Kentucky Derby Pie an easy-to-eat twist by making a tasty bar version. It's full of crunchy pecans and chocolate flavor with a flaky crust. For an extra nod to the "Run for the Roses," simple vanilla cupcakes topped with piped red frosting roses are easy to prepare a day in advance or to order from a local bakery. These are an especially popular hit with the kids if you have little ones at your Derby festivities.

PASTRY CRUST

1 cup cold butter

1 cup all-purpose flour

2 tablespoons half-and-half

$^1/_2$ teaspoon salt

CHOCOLATE PECAN FILLING

$1^1/_2$ cups firmly packed light brown sugar

1 cup unsalted butter

$^1/_2$ cup honey

$^1/_3$ cup sugar

$^1/_4$ cup heavy cream

4 cups pecan halves, divided

1 cup semisweet chocolate chips

PASTRY CRUST

In a mixing bowl, use a pastry blender or the back of a fork to cut the cold butter into the flour. Add half-and-half and salt and blend into a ball of dough. Line a 9 x 13-inch pan with parchment paper and press pastry crust into bottom of pan. Refrigerate while preparing the filling.

CHOCOLATE PECAN FILLING

Preheat oven to 350° F. Prepare filling by combining brown sugar, butter, honey, sugar, and heavy cream in a saucepan over medium heat. Bring to a boil, stirring constantly for 3–4 minutes. Remove from heat and stir in 3 cups of pecans and the chocolate chips. Pour over pastry crust in the pan. Top with remaining 1 cup of pecan halves. Bake for 25–30 minutes. Allow to cool, refrigerate for 1 hour, and then cut into squares.

YIELD: 12 3-INCH SQUARES

Drink

The Derby is all about bourbon, so be sure to have a variety on hand, including a few of the classic Kentucky bourbons like Woodford Reserve and Maker's Mark. Set it up bar style for guests to make their own mint julep. Place extra roses in mint julep–style vases around your main party table and any bar carts.

Classic Mint Julep

1 ounce mint simple syrup (recipe below)

2 ounces bourbon

Mint sprig, for garnish

Fill a silver julep cup with crushed ice. Add mint simple syrup and bourbon. Garnish with a sprig of mint.

YIELD: 1 MINT JULEP

Alongside the main party table, my grandmother's antique wicker tea cart served as the perfect mint julep station.

Mint Simple Syrup

20 stalks of mint

2 cups sugar

2 cups water

Heat the sugar and water in a saucepan and bring to a boil. Remove from the heat and let cool slightly. Pour over the mint and let set, refrigerated, in a jug (pottery) for 24 hours. Pour this solution through a strainer and refrigerate in airtight container until needed.

YIELD: 2 1/2 CUPS

 TIP: *Use extra fabric from your tablecloth to create your own coordinating tea towels or napkins.*

Frozen Mint Julep Punch

It's not a Kentucky Derby party without mint juleps, so in addition to the classic cocktail, a Frozen Mint Julep Punch is a must-have. The fabulous thing about this recipe is that you can prepare and freeze it prior to the party—just scoop and serve as guests arrive!

1 (12-ounce) can frozen lemonade concentrate, thawed and undiluted

1 (12-ounce) can limeade concentrate, thawed and undiluted

1 cup Mint Simple Syrup (page 44)

2 cups water

2 cups bourbon

Combine ingredients and stir well. Freeze in a large container and scoop into mint julep cups to serve.

YIELD: 8–10 SERVINGS

 TIP: *Consider growing your own mint. It's an easy herb to grow and you'll use it often. I have several mint varieties growing in pots in my backyard.*

DIY Favor: Mint Julep To Go

Send your party guests home with their own Mint Julep To Go. Fill a faux silver julep cup (often used for floral decorating) with party filler and top with a mini bottle of bourbon and a mini bottle of homemade simple syrup. Add in a horseshoe stir stick, ribbon stir stick, and finish with a ribbon bow tie on the cup. Display on your party table or small side table as guests leave.

Create

DIY: Grass Centerpiece

Plastic liner

All-purpose potting soil

Rye grass seed

Fill your plastic liner with potting soil. Add water to moisten and then sprinkle generously with grass seed. Rye grass seeds grow very well in 10–12 days if watered daily and placed in a sunny location.

 TIP: *Pick a plastic liner that fits easily into your container for the table. For example, we chose liners that were roughly the same size as the trays we placed them in.*

Birthday Celebration for Her

MY ABSOLUTE FAVORITE OCCASION TO CELEBRATE!

I'm not sure why actual birthday parties seem to phase out after age sixteen, but it's high time they make a resurgence. Ignore the number and focus on the party, or at least the cocktails! Celebrate a girlfriend with the ultimate present: a gathering of her best friends around a festive tablescape.

Whenever I'm searching for the ultimate tablecloth (sometimes white just won't do), I remember my favorite party resource: the fabric store. Fabric designs often come in complementary patterns that work beautifully for tablecloths and coordinating napkins. I chose a vibrant raspberry hue for this birthday fête.

Long-stemmed cocktail glasses make everyone feel fancy. Even if you're serving non-alcoholic punch, jazz it up with festive glassware.

Embellish the simple place settings by adding custom calligraphy wooden place cards atop simple dinnerware. I chose an acrylic paint in a similar raspberry color to paint the laser-cut names. Check our Resources section (page 194) for laser cutting shops.

The easiest way to embellish a table for a variety of different themes is to utilize white dinnerware. Then you can add a paper detail, wooden name card, or other unique touch to tie into your theme.

Square glass vases sprayed white and filled with a variety of roses and other blooms in the color palette of raspberry pink, peach, and orange hues make a simple yet stately centerpiece. It's also a perfect gift for the birthday girl to take home after the party.

Eat

Whether you make everything from scratch or add a homemade appetizer to a catered lunch (totally allowed), keep it light and colorful. Jazz up typical favorites like caprese salad by giving it a tropical twist. Utilize white serving dishes and cake stands to make the food pop!

Peach Pineapple Caprese Skewers

2 peaches

2 cups cubed pineapple (1-inch pieces)

4 ounces fresh mozzarella, cut into cubes

12 small basil leaves

$\frac{1}{8}$ cup balsamic glaze

Slice peaches into small wedges and cut each wedge in half to create 2 small triangles. Layer a bamboo skewer with peach, basil leaf, mozzarella, and finish with pineapple so that the skewer will sit flat. Serve alongside balsamic glaze.

YIELD: 12 SKEWERS

TIP: *For a taller cake, double the recipe to create four layers. You can also slice one layer into two thin layers if you want a thin-layered cake.*

Almond Buttercream Birthday Cake

Dessert should be included on the party table instead of hiding in the kitchen. It helps add to décor and gets everyone quite excited about cake! You can easily add sparklers to a birthday cake like we did on our Crêpe Cake (see page 101). I also love to use extra tall and skinny taper candles as birthday candles for extra pizzazz.

CAKE

1 cup butter

3 cups sugar

1 cup sour cream

1 cup milk

3 eggs, room temperature

3 cups, plus 6 tablespoons cake flour

1 teaspoon salt

1½ tablespoons almond extract

½ teaspoon lemon extract

ALMOND BUTTERCREAM FROSTING

4 ounces cream cheese

½ cup butter

3½ cups powdered sugar

1 tablespoon milk

1 tablespoon almond extract

½ teaspoon lemon extract

CAKE

Preheat oven to 350° F. In the bowl of an electric mixer, beat the butter and sugar until well blended. Add the sour cream and milk and continue beating. Next add the eggs, one at a time, beating after each addition. Add the flour, salt, and almond and lemon extracts and beat until well combined. Bake in two 8- or 9-inch round baking pans sprayed with nonstick cooking spray for 40–45 minutes, or until a toothpick inserted comes out clean.

ALMOND BUTTERCREAM FROSTING

Soften the cream cheese and butter (if not already at room temperature), in the microwave for 10 seconds. Add the powdered sugar and beat with an electric mixer. Next add the milk, almond extract, and lemon extract and beat until fluffy.

ASSEMBLY

Assemble the cake by spreading frosting between the layers and thinly over the outside of the cake. Right before serving, press clipped roses or other flowers into the top to create a floral topping. Store in the refrigerator until ready to serve. If preparing in advance, place flower buds into floral tubes and carefully insert into the top of the cake.

YIELD: 1 (8- OR 9-INCH) CAKE

Drink

Sometimes the simplest of cocktails creates a dynamite birthday toast when served in gold-rimmed champagne coupes. This pink lemonade punch is a favorite at all my parties. Put your own twist on it by experimenting with juice flavors or serving it blended for a frozen treat.

Pink Lemonade Punch Cocktail

1 (12-ounce) can pink lemonade concentrate, thawed and undiluted

2 cups water

1½ cups vodka

1 cup cranberry juice

½ cup orange liqueur

Combine pink lemonade concentrate, water, vodka, cranberry juice, and orange liqueur in a large pitcher. Stir well and store in the refrigerator until ready to serve.

YIELD: 6–8 COCKTAILS

 TIP: *Add a scoop of strawberry sorbet or ice cream to the cocktail glass before pouring in the drink. Serve with a spoon for a "cocktail float."*

Create

While party stores usually only carry basic colored party hats and horns, you can give them a designer feel with a little crafting. We wrapped plain party horns to create custom party horns that add a lot of flair to the table! Even adults' parties look more festive with party hats and horns.

DIY Custom Party Horns

Plain party horns

1 (6 x 7-inch) piece of fabric, multiplied by number of party horns

1 can spray adhesive

Hot glue gun and hot glue sticks

Remove the tips of the party horns and set aside. Carefully unroll one of the horns to use as a pattern for cutting the fabric. Cut out as many pieces of the fabric from this pattern as you need to create your party horns. You can then re-glue the horn you used as your pattern. Spray the horns with adhesive spray and wrap the fabric around the horn. Work fast as the spray adhesive does dry quickly. If needed, trim the fabric to even out edges. Carefully add the tips of the horns back onto the fabric horns using a small amount of hot glue.

A Modern May Day Lunch

"Making your guests feel at home is truly an art and it's one worth cultivating." —Kate Spade

A traditional spring observance noted for singing, dancing, and eating cake, May Day is an ancient Northern Hemisphere holiday, and astronomically, it falls halfway between the spring equinox and the summer solstice. Festivals mark the day where maypoles are wrapped with colorful ribbons, and homemade May baskets are filled with spring flowers and left on doorsteps. May Day is the perfect transition into the warmer days of spring and a wonderful opportunity to set up an outdoor lunch or dinner with friends. You'll find lots of modern May Day touches in this colorful backyard soirée. Don't hold back with your color palette for a May Day affair: take advantage of vibrant peaches, pinks, and aquas.

This is a holiday noted for its bright colors, so I incorporated them from the maypole centerpiece to the individual lunch baskets.

When serving a basic salad like a mixed fruit salad, give it a little pizzazz by serving it in a citrus bowl. It adds extra flavor and a pop of color. Simply halve a large fruit (such as an orange or grapefruit) and hollow out the insides. Fill with your salad and garnish with a sprig of mint.

 TIP: *Many of these sweet party details would be very fitting for baby or bridal showers as well.*

Floral elements are everywhere from the pink peonies topping each napkin to the individual bottles of rose lemonade. You'll also find Sugared Rose Petals (see page 72) atop mini cakes for dessert.

While it might be difficult to visit the doors of all your friends to surprise them with a May Day basket, you can easily create a mini version as the perfect party favor. Individual mini vases tied off with colorful ribbon are filled with a variety of fragrant flowers for this nearly effortless gift.

Eat

Keep in mind that you don't have to use a plate for a place setting. Get creative with mini baskets, mini buckets, flower pot saucers, or other containers that are especially suitable for outdoor affairs.

Hot Chicken Salad

4 cups cooked chicken (bite-sized chunks)

3 cups chopped celery,

$1/2$ cup almonds, toasted and chopped

3 tablespoons chopped onion

2 tablespoons lemon juice

$1/4$ teaspoon pepper

$1/4$ teaspoon red pepper

$1/2$ teaspoon salt

$1^1/2$ cups mayonnaise

1 cup stuffed olives, chopped (optional)

2 (8-ounce) cans sliced water chestnuts, drained

3 cups grated sharp cheddar cheese, divided, plus more if desired

Preheat oven to 350° F. Mix all the ingredients together except 1 cup of cheese. Pour into a greased 9 x 13-inch casserole dish. Top with the 1 remaining cup of cheese (add more cheese as desired). Bake for 30 minutes.

YIELD: 10–12 SERVINGS

TIP: *Instead of minis, create one large rose cake; this would also be beautiful served as a birthday cake.*

Mini Rose Cakes

OLD-FASHIONED POUND CAKE

1½ cups butter, softened

3 cups sugar

5 eggs, room temperature

3 cups all-purpose flour

1 teaspoon salt

1 cup milk

2 teaspoons vanilla extract

Preheat oven to 350° F. In a mixing bowl, use an electric mixer to beat the butter and sugar until fluffy. Next, add the eggs and beat until well combined. Then add the flour, salt, milk, and vanilla. Beat for 5 minutes. Pour into a 9 x 13-inch baking pans sprayed with nonstick cooking spray. Bake for 40–45 minutes or until a toothpick inserted comes out clean. Cool in the baking pan for five minutes. Use a round cookie cutter or biscuit cutter to cut out 24 cake rounds.

PINK BUTTERCREAM FROSTING

1 cup unsalted butter, softened

3–4 cups powdered sugar

¼ teaspoon salt

1 tablespoon vanilla extract

3 tablespoons milk or heavy cream

2 drops pink food coloring

In the bowl of an electric mixer, beat butter for 2 minutes on medium speed. Adjust speed to low and add powdered sugar, 1 cup at a time. Add salt, vanilla, milk, and food coloring. Beat on medium for 3 minutes. Add additional powdered sugar for a thicker consistency or more milk for a thinner consistency. Add more or less pink food coloring until you achieve your desired color.

Layer mini pound cake rounds with buttercream frosting. Top with sugared rose petals.

YIELD: 12 MINI CAKES

HINTS FOR COOKING POUND CAKES

1. To measure the flour and sugar, spoon into measuring cup and then level using the straight edge of a knife. Do not pack flour.

2. Remove the eggs and butter from the refrigerator about two hours or the night before making the cake so that each is at room temperature.

Sugared Rose Petals

2 rose buds, just blooming

$^1/_2$ cup granulated sugar

1 cup powdered sugar

1$^1/_2$ teaspoons meringue powder

3 tablespoons water

Be sure to select only organically grown roses (no pesticides). Each rose bud will produce about 15 petals. Peel petals off, rinse, and lay flat to dry. Use a food processor to pulse the granulated sugar until consistency is very fine. In a blender, combine powdered sugar, meringue powder, and water and pulse until smooth. Beat on high speed for 4–5, minutes or until fluffy. Dip one petal at a time into the meringue mixture, covering both sides. Next, dip petals into superfine sugar, coating both sides. Place on baking sheet lined with wax paper. Let dry at room temperature for 2 hours, and then turn the petals over to continue drying overnight. Store the sugared petals in an airtight container with wax paper between the layers of petals.

TIP: *Since roses are edible, you can also float petals or mini buds down in cocktails or salads for a fancy garnish. Other edible flowers: carnations, impatiens, lilacs, marigolds, violets, and pansies.*

Drink

Rose Lemonade Cocktail

5 ounces Fentimans Rose Lemonade

1¹⁄₂ ounces vodka

1 tablespoon lemon juice

Combine rose lemonade, vodka, and lemon juice and pour over ice.

If you cannot locate Rose Lemonade, alternate with 4 ounces lemonade and 1 ounce of rose syrup (recipe below).

YIELD: 1 COCKTAIL

Rose Syrup

1 cup sugar

1 cup water

2 cups rose petals, organically grown (no pesticides)

Combine sugar and water in a saucepan over medium heat until sugar is dissolved. Reduce heat to low, add rose petals, and let simmer on low for 30 minutes, stirring occasionally. Allow to cool and strain to use or store.

YIELD: 1¹⁄₂ CUPS

Create

Even if you aren't super crafty, a little ribbon and hot glue go a long way! Whether you want to create a colorful maypole centerpiece or just jazz up simple vases for party favors (see page 67), adding a DIY touch really gives your party a custom feel.

DIY: Maypole Centerpiece

Flower pot

Styrofoam cut to fit into the circumference of your pot

$\frac{1}{2}$-inch x 15-inch wooden dowel

Hot glue gun and hot glue sticks

Satin ribbon in assorted colors, $\frac{1}{2}$-inch wide

Silk flower

Secure the Styrofoam in the pot and gently push the wooden dowel into the middle of the Styrofoam until secure.

Cut ribbons to desired length (roughly 16–20 inches, depending on size of table). Hot glue the end of the ribbon pieces on top of the wooden dowel. Lastly, hot glue a silk flower to add to the topper.

 TIP: *Want to jazz up your pot or add more color? Spray paint your wooden dowel and pot to coordinate with your tablecloth and dishes.*

Wedding Anniversary Party

FROM THE FIRST TO THE FIFTIETH, AND BEYOND!

Make an anniversary celebration a memorable affair with lots of DIY touches and personalized party décor. Silver is used for both tenth and twenty-fifth wedding anniversaries, so it's one we wanted to highlight. A silver table covering with a bit of sheen reflects beautifully under the lights. Create a photo booth wall that doubles as party décor by hanging a Mylar silver foil curtain down from the main wall behind your party table. Carry this idea over to the tablescape itself by stringing silver curling ribbon down from the chandelier and out onto the ends of the table. That's a little party trick that my mother did for every birthday party.

Personalize your party by creating simple labels for mini champagne bottles. Measure the dimensions of the bottle's label and create your own, printed on sticker paper. Cut, peel, and place over the original label. I chose to highlight the number twenty-five, but you could create individual labels to serve as place cards as well.

It's easy and beautiful to create a glowing atmosphere with lots of silver taper candles, especially if you're celebrating over dinner. Before lighting candles, trim the wicks to a quarter inch for a better flame. Be sure to keep garlands and ribbon away from the flames.

Frame wedding pictures of the couple in silver frames (or gold for a fiftieth anniversary party) around the table for guests to enjoy. You could even encourage guests to send in favorite pictures of the couple from years past.

Set out a bowl or tray to collect cards and mementos for the special couple. This will help ensure nothing gets lost in the mix, and it's easy to package up at the end of the evening.

 TIP: *For a unique color scheme, look back to the couple's own wedding colors or their flowers.*

DID YOU KNOW *that each wedding anniversary has a corresponding color and traditional gift idea? Check the list below for some of the top anniversaries and their themes. This can provide a starting point for your color palette and overall motif.*

1st Wedding Anniversary:
Color: Yellow
Theme/Gift: Paper

5th Wedding Anniversary:
Color: Blue
Theme/Gift: Wood

10th Wedding Anniversary:
Color: Silver
Theme/Gift: Tin

15th Wedding Anniversary:
Color: Ruby Red
Theme/Gift: Crystal

*20*th **Wedding Anniversary:**
Color: Emerald
Theme/Gift: China

*25*th **Wedding Anniversary:**
Color: Silver
Theme/Gift: Silver

*50*th **Wedding Anniversary:**
Color: Gold
Theme/Gift: Gold

*60*th **and 75th Wedding Anniversaries:**
Color: Diamond White
Theme/Gift: Diamonds

Eat

You'll see silver leaf used twice in the recipes for this anniversary affair. Rest assured it is fully edible and one of my favorite ways of giving food and drink a special touch. While in Paris a couple of years ago, I noted how pastry chefs added a hint of edible gold leaf to almost every sweet treat. I've been hooked on edible gold and silver leaf ever since. A little touch goes a long way.

White Chocolate Cherries

- **1 cup white chocolate chips, or chopped white chocolate or almond bark**
- **1 teaspoon vegetable oil**
- **2 pints stemmed cherries**
- **1 sheet edible silver foil**

Using a microwave or double boiler, melt white chocolate until smooth. Add in vegetable oil and stir. (The oil helps thin the white chocolate as well as give it a nice sheen.) Holding each cherry by the stem, simply dip them into the white chocolate, coating evenly, and place on a wax paper–lined baking sheet to cool. While cooling, quickly dab a small piece of silver foil onto the white chocolate. Allow to fully cool and serve.

YIELD: ABOUT 4 CUPS CHERRIES

Edible Cracker Spoons

2 cups all-purpose flour

1 teaspoon salt

1 teaspoon sugar

²/₃ cup water

¹/₃ cup olive oil

1 tablespoon sea salt

Cream cheese, for garnish

Hot pepper jelly, for garnish

14–16 small basil leaves, for garnish

TIP: *Add ¹/₂ cup of grated cheese, 1 tablespoon of poppy seeds, or additional seasonings to the dough for a variety of crackers.*

Preheat oven to 400° F. Combine flour, salt, and sugar in a mixing bowl. Add in water and olive oil. Stir until combined and a dough is formed. Using a floured surface, roll out dough until ¹/₈ inch thick. Using a spoon-shaped cookie cutter, cut out spoons and carefully place them on a parchment-lined baking sheet. Sprinkle with sea salt and bake for 12–15 minutes. Oven temperatures can vary so remove from oven when crackers are lightly golden.

Garnish it: Top each spoon with a dollop of cream cheese and hot pepper jelly. Garnish with a mini basil leaf.

YIELD: 14–16 CRACKER SPOONS

Drink

You can certainly opt for classic champagne for any and all wedding anniversaries—but if you want to jazz it up, serve something fitting for the number of years being celebrated. Whether you float edible flowers or a touch of silver leaf, there are lots of ways to say, "Sip, sip hooray!"

Silver-Frosted Cocktail

- **2 ounces gin**
- **2 ounces club soda**
- **1 ounce simple syrup**
- **1 tablespoon lemon juice**
- **Edible silver leaf, for garnish**

Combine gin, club soda, simple syrup, and lemon juice in a cocktail shaker filled with ice. Shake vigorously and pour into glass. Garnish with a touch of edible silver leaf.

YIELD: 1 COCKTAIL

 TIP: *Rim glasses in sugar for a sweet touch! I use Wilton's White Sparkling Sugar Sprinkles.*

Create

These sweet cake boxes were the favors at my own wedding. Add to each place setting and fill with mints, chocolates, or a special little treat. Miniature wedding cakes are a work of art that can be saved for years in an airtight container.

DIY: Miniature Wedding Cake Boxes

1 recipe Gum Paste (page 89) or (24-ounce) box white fondant

2$^1/_2$ cups Royal Icing Glue (page 89)

1$^1/_2$-inch and 3-inch cookie cutters

Cardboard paper

Create a pattern by cutting an 8 $^3/_4$-inch long by 1-inch wide pattern and a 4 $^1/_2$-inch long by $^1/_2$-inch wide pattern out of cardboard paper.

Dust your working area with powdered sugar or cornstarch. Roll out gum paste (or fondant) to $^1/_4$ inch thick.

Cut out fourteen 1$^1/_2$-inch circles of gum paste and twenty-eight 3-inch circles of gum paste.

Allow gum paste circles to dry on parchment paper for several hours, or overnight.

When ready to assemble the cakes, use the pattern to cut out fourteen 4$^1/_2$-inch strips and fourteen 8$^3/_4$-inch strips of gum paste. Keep covered with cloth until needed.

To assemble the cakes, moisten the edges of one 1$^1/_2$-inch circle and then moisten the edge of one

4$^1/_2$-inch strip with a little water; form the strip upright around the circle. Place this cake topper on the center of one of the 3-inch circles, and moisten with water to help hold the circle in place. Complete 14 of these cake top lids and let dry.

To assemble the bottom of the cake, moisten the edges of one of the 3-inch circles and the edge of one 8$^3/_4$-inch strip with a little water; form the upright strip around the circle. (Use little aluminum foil balls to support the sides if they sag.) Continue assembling the containers until 14 have been completed and let dry overnight. Do not place the lids on the containers until both are completely dry.

Pipe the edges of the lids and base of the containers using Royal Icing Glue and the decorator tip of your choice. Let the iced containers dry overnight. Place the lids on top of the container after filling the bottom container with mints or small candies.

YIELD: 14 MINIATURE WEDDING CAKE BOXES

TIP: *Gum paste is sugar dough that can be rolled thin and cut with cookie cutters. It dries very hard and looks almost like porcelain. Decorator fondant (white vanilla) can be found at most craft stores and works well in lieu of gum paste if you are in a hurry. It takes a little longer to dry.*

Gum Paste

- **3 (.25-ounce) envelopes unflavored gelatin**
- **1 cup warm water**
- **¹/₂ cup cornstarch**
- **3 (16-ounce) packages powdered sugar**

Mix the gelatin and warm water in a small bowl and let stand for 5 minutes. Then press mixture through a fine strainer into a large mixing bowl. Add cornstarch and beat until smooth. Next add the sugar, 1 cup at a time, until smooth and sticky dough is formed. Place the dough in an airtight container or a large bowl covered with a damp towel.

When working with this dough, use only a small amount at a time. Be sure to keep the remaining dough covered at all times. It dries very quickly. Before rolling the dough out as required for the DIY: Miniature Wedding Cake Boxes, dust it and the work area with extra cornstarch. Gum paste projects can be made ahead of time and stored in a covered box in a dry place.

YIELD: 1 POUND

Royal Icing Glue

- **2 large egg whites, or ¹/₃ cup liquid egg whites**
- **1 tablespoon water**
- **1 (1-pound) package powdered sugar**

Beat egg whites and water until foamy. Add sugar and beat until fluffy with soft peaks. Beat for an additional 4–5 minutes after soft peaks form. If icing is not stiff enough, just add a little more sugar. If too stiff, add a little water, 1 teaspoon at a time. Since it dries quickly, keep the icing covered with a damp cloth while working.

YIELD: 2 ½ CUPS ICING GLUE

Bastille Day Fête

WHAT BETTER WAY TO ENJOY A BIT OF PARISIAN CULTURE?

A few years ago, I had the privilege of spending Bastille Day (July 14th) in Paris, France, with my mother. We gallivanted around the city and enjoyed dinner while watching the fireworks above the Eiffel Tower. It was the trip of a lifetime! We came back with a newfound respect for Bastille Day after seeing all the festivities. You'll certainly find lots of red, white, and blue inspiration for American, Australian, and English patriotic holidays as well!

A large Eiffel Tower makes the perfect centerpiece.

We kept the rest of the décor simple, like placing French lemonade bottles down the table and putting mini red vases with French flags at each setting as a simple favor.

TIP: *A long charcuterie board would be a very fitting centerpiece as well. See this idea on display in the Book Club Gathering chapter (page 105).*

Twinkling cafe lights and simple red fabric bunting garlands were hung around the party table.

While we couldn't enjoy actual fireworks over the Eiffel Tower at our party, presenting the crêpe cake topped with sparklers was the ultimate encore to our dinner.

TIP: *A dusting of powdered sugar atop any dessert gives it a fancy finish!*

Eat

After tasting macarons at every corner in Paris, we knew they had to make an appearance: simple store-bought macarons brushed with diluted food coloring created the perfect sweet treat for guests to enjoy.

For the savory side, guests were greeted with a mini baguette and place card atop their salad plate. In Paris, I fell in love with amazing French cheeses and breads, so we created a mini cheese board for guests.

 TIP: *For a simple favor idea, package up a few macarons in a cellophane bag or a little box tied up with a red or blue bow.*

Arugula Salad

4 cups baby arugula leaves, rinsed and dried

$\frac{1}{2}$ cup candied walnuts

$\frac{1}{2}$ cup dried cranberries

$\frac{1}{4}$ cup crumbled blue cheese

3 tablespoons fig balsamic vinaigrette

Toss the walnuts, cranberries, and blue cheese crumbles with arugula leaves. Drizzle with fig balsamic vinaigrette and enjoy.

YIELD: 4 SIDE SALADS

Tomato Crostini

24 baguette slices

4 ounces chèvre (goat) cheese

1 pint cherry tomatoes, thinly sliced

Toast baguette slices until golden brown. Spread with chèvre and top with sliced tomatoes.

YIELD: 24 CROSTINI

 TIP: *To give your appetizers that finishing touch, keep fresh herbs on hand. A sprig of dill or mini basil leaf is the perfect accompaniment to crostini, canapés, and small bites.*

Crêpe Cake

4 cups all-purpose flour

8 eggs

2 cups milk

2 cups water

1 teaspoon salt

1 teaspoon vanilla extract

½ cup butter, melted

Whisk together flour and eggs in large mixing bowl. Slowly add in milk and water, whisking to combine until smooth. Add salt, vanilla, and butter. Beat with the whisk until combined.

Heat an oiled frying pan on medium heat. Prepare crêpes with ¼ cup batter a piece and tilt pan in a circular motion to fully coat the bottom. Cook for 2 minutes on each side, or until lightly golden. Remove from heat and prepare next crêpe.

Stack each crêpe with a spoonful of lemon sauce between each layer.

YIELD: 1 CRÊPE CAKE (FOR A TALLER CAKE, DOUBLE OR TRIPLE THE RECIPE)

Lemon Sauce for Crêpe Cake

2 cups sugar

1 cup butter

⅔ cup fresh lemon juice

4 large eggs, slightly beaten

¼ cup lemon zest

Combine sugar, butter, and lemon juice in the top of a double boiler. Once the water starts to boil, reduce the heat to low and cook until the butter melts. Remove from the stove, cool slightly (about 15 minutes), and then gradually stir in eggs, 1 at a time, stirring constantly. Return to medium heat, stirring constantly, until the mixture thickens and coats a spoon; 15–20 minutes. Remove from heat and cool. Strain sauce and stir in lemon zest. Allow to cool and refrigerate, covered. Store lemon sauce in an airtight container in the refrigerator for up to one week.

YIELD: 2 ¼ CUPS LEMON SAUCE

 TIP: *Microwave lemons for 30 seconds to get more juice.*

Drink

Wine and prosecco are a must at Bastille Day parties, but it's not a Pizzazzerie party without a cocktail that fits the celebration. Liven up prosecco with fresh raspberry puree and a touch of sugar. Or create a prosecco bar with a variety of fruity mix-ins for your guests to enjoy!

Sparkling Raspberry Cocktail

1 cup fresh raspberries

1 tablespoon sugar

1 (750 ml) bottle prosecco

Puree raspberries with sugar until well blended. Strain through a sieve to remove any seeds. Spoon several tablespoons of puree into the bottom of 4 cocktail glasses. Top with prosecco.

YIELD: 4 COCKTAILS

 TIP: *A multitude of different bottle labels can often make a tablescape feel "busy," so I like to pour wine into glass carafes.*

Book Club Gathering

"A party without cake is just a meeting."
—Julia Child

Book clubs are making quite the comeback, and why not? A chance to enjoy quality conversation over a recent read and indulge in delicious food? Count me in! While many of us likely won't pull out the fine china for a book club party, the occasion certainly warrants a celebratory affair.

Set your table in style and impress your guests with this unique tablescape. Create a custom place mat for your book club meeting by printing an image of the book's cover. You can often find this online or even snap a picture of the cover yourself. Have it printed on 11 x 14-inch paper at an office supply or printing store. This is an easy and inexpensive touch that not only creates quite the conversation piece but also makes clean up a breeze.

Wrap a simple vase in vintage book pages and tie off with twine. Also, add sprigs of lavender and mint to the food and drink displays for an extra touch of fancy.

Little wooden letters from the craft store spelled out "book club" at our party, but you can spell out the book's title as well.

Each guest had her very own mini wooden board instead of a traditional plate. Think outside the box when setting the table; you don't always have to use plates!

Send guests home with a themed favor like miniature recipe books! Or find a little gift that fits the theme of the book you're discussing. You certainly don't have to present a favor, but it always make guests feel special to leave with a little something fun.

Eat

Even if you're not serving a full lunch or dinner, sitting around a table enjoying light bites and appetizers is the perfect arrangement for your book club conversations. To encourage the "togetherness" feeling even further, I opted for a single long charcuterie board full of delicious foods. Select easy-to-eat items like fruits, cheeses, olives, nuts, tea sandwiches, and cheddar biscuits. Consider tailoring your menu to your book's theme and printing the menu to resemble a library card.

Mini Cheddar Biscuits

2 cups all-purpose flour

$\frac{1}{4}$ teaspoon salt

$\frac{1}{8}$ teaspoon red pepper

1 cup sharp cheddar cheese

1 cup heavy cream

Preheat oven to 450° F. Mix the flour, salt, and red pepper until well blended. Add the cheese and cream and mix again until combined. Round dough out on a floured board. Using a $1\frac{1}{2}$-inch cutter, cut the biscuits, and then place them on a parchment-lined cookie sheet. Brush tops with melted butter or milk and bake for 10–12 minutes.

YIELD: 42 BISCUITS

Rinne's Spinach Tea Sandwiches

1 (10-ounce) package frozen chopped spinach

2 cups mayonnaise

$\frac{1}{2}$ cup dried minced onion

$\frac{1}{2}$ cup dried parsley

1 tablespoon fresh lemon juice

2 drops hot sauce

1 large loaf sliced wheat bread

Cook the spinach according to the directions on the package. Drain well to remove all excess moisture, and then pat with paper towels. Combine the spinach with the mayonnaise, onion, parsley, lemon juice, and hot sauce and mix well. Cover and refrigerate the mixture for 2–3 hours, allowing the flavors to blend.

Spread the spinach mixture on half the slices of bread and top with the remaining slices. Refrigerate for several hours, and then trim crusts from the slices of bread (it makes a cleaner cut when cold). Cut each sandwich into quarters. Store in a covered container in refrigerator.

YIELD: ABOUT 48 TEA SANDWICHES

HINTS FOR TEA SANDWICHES

1. Consider using one dark and one light slice of bread for both taste and presentation.

2. Mince, chop, and grind ingredients for ease of eating.

3. Spread filling all the way to the edge to prevent dry edges.

Mini Blueberry Shortcakes

½ cup butter, melted

1 (16-ounce) box pound cake mix

4 eggs, divided

8 ounces cream cheese, softened

1 (1-pound) package powdered sugar

2 cups whipped topping

½ cup blueberry jam

Fresh blueberries

Fresh mint sprigs, for garnish

Preheat oven to 350° F.

Combine butter, pound cake mix, and 2 eggs.
Stir until combined. Press the thick batter
mixture evenly into a 9 x 13-inch greased
baking pan.

With an electric mixer, beat cream cheese,
remaining 2 eggs, and powdered sugar until
fluffy. Spread batter over cake mixture, being
sure to spread evenly to the edges of the pan.
Bake for 45 minutes, or until lightly golden.
Cool and cut into desired shapes to fit your
serving container.

Mix the whipped topping and blueberry jam
until well blended. Top each shortcake with a
dollop of cream mixture, sprinkle with fresh
blueberries, and garnish with sprigs of mint.

YIELD: 9 MINI SHORTCAKES

 TIP: *Stack old books to raise your charcuterie board and tie into the theme of your party.*

Drink

At our *Pride and Prejudice* book club party, guests enjoyed proper Lavender Fizz Cocktails. If you want to avoid alcohol, serve up festive mocktails from fresh juices to spritzers made with club soda. Always be sure to have water on hand too.

Lavender Fizz Cocktail

- **2 ounces gin**
- **1 ounce fresh lemon juice**
- **1 ounce Lavender Simple Syrup (recipe follows)**
- **1 ounce club soda**
- **Fresh lavender sprigs, for garnish**

Combine gin, lemon juice, and Lavender Simple Syrup in a shaker filled with ice. Shake vigorously and strain over ice. Finish with club soda. Garnish with a sprig of lavender.

YIELD: 1 COCKTAIL

Lavender Simple Syrup

- **1 cup sugar**
- **1 cup water**
- **2 tablespoons dried lavender**

Combine sugar and water in a medium saucepan over medium heat. Bring to a boil and stir until sugar is dissolved. Remove from heat and add lavender. Allow to cool and refrigerate overnight. Strain to remove lavender buds.

YIELD: 1½ CUPS

A Dapper Birthday Celebration for Him

PUT YOUR TWIST ON IT!

As a blogger and stylist, I have a strong pulse on the parties and ideas that people search for online. One of these types of parties is birthday party ideas for the guys in their life. While the days of staying out at the bars until the wee hours might be long gone, birthdays are still worth celebrating. So if you're looking to throw your special guy a birthday party that's still manly and acceptable among all his friends, we've got you covered.

I hosted a dapper birthday bash in rustic browns and hunter-greens, and incorporated lots of favorite guy-foods. For more ideas, consider throwing him a Mexican-themed bash: get your inspiration from our Día de los Muertos Fiesta (page 159) and switch up the mini bottle favors to tequila. Or take a cue from the Book Club Gathering (page 105), by integrating his favorite sci-fi novels or classic authors into the theme. Tailor it to *your* dapper gentleman's favorite foods and drinks to truly make it a special birthday to remember.

A rustic farm setting was the perfect location for a hunter-green color palette filled with details from dapper stir sticks to belt buckle napkin rings. Find inspiration and pick a few details to recreate for your guy's birthday.

Visit local cigar stores and ask for cigar boxes to create stacks down the center of the table. Grab a variety of beer bottles and growlers to use as vases for simple greenery and even hops!

Instead of traditional chargers, wooden rounds give the table a unique, rustic touch. Display a variety of bottles (in our case, Scotch and whiskey) as a casual tasting while they enjoy dinner. Print off simple "tasting notes" and place beside each setting.

 TIP: *Simple green wrapping paper wrapped with natural raffia ribbon keeps presents festive and fitting for a guy's party.*

Solid-green napkins wrapped with old belts create the perfect DIY napkin ring; check your local thrift store to find old belts. And as always, send your party guests home with a few items they'll love—like cigars and mini bottles of Scotch or whiskey.

Dress up the drinks as well with custom "dapper" stir sticks. Use ribbon or fabric to create bow ties to add to liquor bottles.

Eat

If your party includes a fireplace or fire pit, s'mores are a no-brainer. Regular s'mores are fine, but for special parties, you must up the ante. I'm talking about Bacon and Pecan S'mores that will wow all your guests.

Bacon and Pecan S'mores

12 graham cracker sheets

$^1/_2$ cup (1 stick) butter

1 cup firmly packed brown sugar

$^1/_2$ cup chopped pecans

$^1/_2$ cup chopped bacon

12 marshmallows, for roasting

6 chocolate bars, broken into squares, for serving

Prepare the graham crackers before the party so all you'll need is the fire to roast your marshmallows.

Preheat oven to 350°F. Line a baking sheet with parchment. Break your graham crackers into square pieces and line up close together on the baking sheet.

In a saucepan, combine butter and brown sugar. Once boiling, remove from heat and pour evenly over graham crackers. Sprinkle the tops of the graham crackers with pecans and bacon. Bake for 10 minutes. Remove from oven and allow to cool.

Prepare s'mores with your bacon and pecan graham crackers, 1 roasted marshmallow, and 1 chocolate square.

YIELD: 12 S'MORES

Sriracha and Bourbon Wings

3 tablespoons vegetable oil

2 pounds chicken wings, split at the joint and tips removed

3 tablespoons unsalted butter, melted

1 clove garlic, minced

$\frac{1}{2}$ teaspoon salt

$\frac{1}{2}$ teaspoon pepper

$\frac{1}{3}$ cup sriracha

$\frac{1}{4}$ cup ketchup

1 teaspoon soy sauce

$\frac{1}{4}$ cup bourbon

$\frac{1}{4}$ cup tomato paste

Ranch or blue cheese dressing, for dipping

Preheat oven to 400° F. Coat a rimmed baking sheet with vegetable oil.

In a bowl, combine wings, butter, garlic, salt, and pepper. Toss to coat. Spread wings onto baking sheet and bake for 40–45 minutes, flipping over halfway through. In a bowl, whisk together sriracha, ketchup, soy sauce, bourbon, and tomato paste. Add in wings and toss to coat. Serve alongside ranch or blue cheese dipping sauce.

YIELD: 18–22 WINGS

TIP: *Serve up wings or other foods in wooden bowls (even wooden salad bowls will work) to complement the rustic elements of this party.*

Candied Bourbon Bacon

12 thick-cut bacon strips

$\frac{1}{2}$ cup firmly packed brown sugar

$\frac{1}{2}$ cup bourbon

$\frac{1}{4}$ cup honey or maple syrup

Preheat oven to 375° F.

Line a baking sheet with parchment paper and place bacon strips on a wire rack placed on top of baking sheet. In a medium saucepan on medium heat, combine brown sugar, bourbon, and honey. Stir to combine and cook down for 15–20 minutes, stirring often. Remove glaze from heat and brush over top of bacon. Bake for 10 minutes.

Remove from oven, flip bacon over, and brush remaining glaze on the other side of bacon strips. Return to oven for 10–12 minutes, or until bacon starts to curl at the ends. Remove from oven, and allow to cool. Bacon will crisp as it cools, but bake for longer if you prefer even crispier bacon.

YIELD: 12 BACON STRIPS

Spicy Sausage Balls

1 pound hot sausage, uncooked

3 cups grated sharp cheddar cheese

3 cups Bisquick

Preheat oven to 400° F.

Crumble the sausage in a bowl with the cheese and let soften to room temperature, or microwave until softened. Combine this mixture thoroughly with Bisquick. Round into 1-inch balls and bake on a parchment-lined baking sheet for 10–12 minutes. Sausage balls are good served cold but even better hot.

YIELD: 76 BALLS

CANDIED BOURBON BACON

SPICY
SAUSAGE
BALLS

TASTING
NOTES

TENNESSEE
ICED WATER

Drink

Tennessee Iced Water

This was the signature cocktail at my wedding, and friends and family are still talking about it. It's a Tennessee favorite!

- 1 ounce citron vodka
- 1 ounce gin

- 4–6 ounces lemon-lime soda
- Splash of lime juice
- Lemon wedge, for garnish

Combine citron vodka, gin, lemon-lime soda, and splash of lime juice. Shake and pour over ice. Garnish with a lemon wedge.

YIELD: 1 COCKTAIL

 TIP: *I love to garnish cocktails with a complementary herb such as a sprig of rosemary seen here or a sprig of lavender (see page 114).*

Spicy Maple Bourbon Cocktail

- Lime juice, for rimming
- Pinch of ancho chile powder, plus more for rimming
- 2 ounces bourbon
- 1½ ounces orange juice
- ½ ounce pure maple syrup
- Orange peel, for garnish

Rim glasses by dipping in lime juice and then a shallow bowl or plate of ancho chile powder. Fill glass with ice. Add in bourbon, orange juice, maple syrup, and a pinch of chile powder. Garnish with an orange peel.

YIELD: 1 COCKTAIL

Autumnal Equinox Party

"Autumn . . . the year's last, loveliest smile."
—William Cullen Bryant

With the cooler weather arriving, it's the perfect opportunity to take the party outside! I first heard of autumnal equinox parties from my best friend who was living in New York City at the time. She annually hosted her friends for a fabulous fête to welcome the change of the seasons. Naturally, this was a party theme I could easily get behind.

Welcome autumn with rich fall hues like copper, chocolate brown, and pops of natural green. Allow the outdoor colors to elevate your party setting by taking the party to the backyard or a park. Create a low table and scatter throw pillows and cozy blankets for guests to sit on.

Beautiful fall leaves scattered with acorns and pinecones create a natural centerpiece that's perfectly fitting for the season. Add in taper candles in wooden candlesticks. Get crafty and spray unfinished wooden candlesticks from the craft store in metallic hues like brass, copper, and gold.

Simple white dinnerware gets an autumn pop with pumpkin-orange monogrammed napkins tied with a stalk of wheat.

TIP: *For seating at a low table, I used 20 x 20-inch pillows as a comfortable "seat" for guests. Add in throw blankets for chilly nights.*

Fill copper and glass vases with scattered leaves and candles. Bring in more of the fall color palette with copper martini glasses and rose gold flatware. Moscow mules would also be a great addition to this party with their copper color.

Use the elements of this Autumnal Equinox Party (along with the recipes) to inspire you for Friendsgiving gatherings, Thanksgiving, fall bridal showers, and any other autumn occasion. The natural elements that enhance this table are easy to pull together for last-minute occasions.

Eat

Look to your season to pull in flavorful favorites, like pumpkin in the fall. Don't stop there—swap traditional serving bowls for actual pumpkins to serve up appetizers, soups, or salads.

Chocolate Almond Acorns

¼ cup semisweet chocolate chips

1 cup whole almonds

¼ cup chocolate sprinkles

Melt chocolate chips and dip the rounded end of each almond into the chocolate. Be sure to cover just the bottom of the almond. Next, dip the chocolate end into chocolate sprinkles. Lay flat on wax paper to dry.

YIELD: 36-48 ALMONDS

Roasted Garlic & Pumpkin Hummus

2 (15.5 ounce) cans chickpeas

1 (15 ounce) can pureed pumpkin

2 tablespoons tahini

3 cloves garlic, roasted

1 teaspoon salt

2 tablespoons lemon juice

1 teaspoon cumin

¼ cup extra virgin olive oil

Pumpkin seed kernels, for garnish

Paprika, for garnish

Combine chickpeas, pumpkin, tahini, garlic, salt, lemon juice, cumin, and olive oil in a food processor. Blend until smooth. Serve garnished with pumpkin seed kernels and a dash of paprika.

YIELD: 3 CUPS

TIP: *I love sending guests home with a favor like pumpkin spice bread. Other homemade favors to try: caramel apples, pumpkin butter, or apple butter.*

David's Pumpkin Spice Bread

This recipe is from my brother, and has been a favorite for years. Find him at SpicedBlog.com!

- **¾ cup oil**
- **4 large eggs**
- **⅔ cup water**
- **1 (15-ounce) canned pumpkin**
- **2½ cups all-purpose flour**
- **3 cups sugar**
- **2 teaspoons baking soda**
- **1 teaspoon salt**
- **1 tablespoon cinnamon**
- **1 tablespoon nutmeg**
- **2 teaspoons cloves**
- **1 teaspoon ginger**

Preheat oven to 350° F.

Combine oil, eggs, water, and pumpkin in a large mixing bowl. Stir well to combine. In separate bowl, combine flour, sugar, baking soda, salt, and spices. Stir to combine. Slowly add the dry ingredients to the wet ingredients and stir fully to combine.

Spray baking pans (mini loaf pans or full-size loaf pans) with nonstick cooking spray. Pour batter into pans. Bake for approximately 35–45 minutes for full loaves, 25 minutes for mini loaves, or until a toothpick inserted into middle of cake comes out clean.

YIELD: 5 MINI LOAVES, 2 FULL-SIZE LOAVES

One Bowl Pumpkin Spice Bread

Pressed for time? Here is a cake mix version.

- **1 (16.5-ounce) box spice cake mix**
- **1 cup pumpkin puree**
- **⅔ cup water**
- **2 eggs, beaten**
- **2 teaspoons cinnamon**
- **½ teaspoon nutmeg**

Preheat oven to 400° F.

Combine cake mix, pumpkin, water, eggs, cinnamon, and nutmeg and beat with electric mixer until well blended.

Spray loaf pan or muffin tin with nonstick cooking spray. Spoon the batter into the loaf pan or tins, and bake for 25 minutes for loaves, 20 minutes for regular muffins, and 15 minutes for mini muffins. Watch closely as cooking time can vary based on pan size and oven. Bread is done when a toothpick inserted into center comes out clean.

YIELD: 1 FULL-SIZE LOAF, 12 REGULAR-SIZED MUFFINS, OR 60 MINI MUFFINS

Drink

Spice up the season with infused flavors from your favorite fall desserts, like caramel apples! Take note that you can easily increase the size of these drink recipes by 6 to 8 to create a pitcher-style beverage.

Caramel Apple Martini

2 ounces apple cider

1 ounce sour apple pucker

1 ounce caramel vodka

Sliced apple and caramel sauce, for garnish

Combine all ingredients in a shaker filled with ice. Shake and pour into a martini glass drizzled with caramel sauce. Garnish with a fresh apple slice.

YIELD: 1 COCKTAIL

Create

Some party crafts last forever. If you love to throw parties, creating a boho dining table is one of the best (and most useful!) things you can make. Use it for everything from backyard gatherings to children's parties.

DIY Low Dining Table

2 (3 x 6-feet) pieces plywood (¼ inch thick)

Wood stain (we used Minwax Special Walnut stain)

Tung oil finish

Wooden crates

Stain your plywood the color of your choice. Let dry overnight. Coat the tops with 1 coat of tung oil finish. Let dry overnight.

To build the low dining table, place wooden boards over crates to create one long low table. You can also use large pots or other similar items to raise the wooden boards. We used 2 wooden crates on each end and 2 in the middle to create a solid support under our boards.

 TIP: *You can certainly create a longer table or shorter table depending on the size of your party.*

Acorn Drink Stirrers

Acorns

Shellac spray or spray paint (optional)

Wooden skewer sticks

Ice pick

If you want your acorns to have a shine to them, then first spray with shellac or clear lacquer. Or paint with a colored spray paint such as gold or copper. This step is optional.

Next, carefully poke a hole into the bottom of the acorn with an ice pick. Try to poke the hole as close to the center of the acorn as possible. Be sure not to poke the hole all the way through to the other side, just a small hole is fine. Slide the wooden skewer into the acorn hole until it fits snugly. Use for drink stirrers or appetizer sticks to dress up cheese or other bite-size foods.

Charleston Garden Party

"Genuine hospitality . . . cannot be described, but is immediately felt." —Washington Irving

If you've ever visited this city of cobblestone streets, horse-drawn carriages, and single houses full of charm, then you'll know what I mean when I say that the city stays with you. From the onset of this book, I knew I wanted to celebrate Charleston with a garden luncheon devoted to all of my favorite elements of this charming coastal city. This is the perfect theme for rehearsal dinners where guests are often from out of town, or for going-away parties.

Growing up in downtown Charleston, I learned the art of entertaining at an early age. Embodying all of Charleston's Southern charm, this garden luncheon touches on my favorite elements of the city. From monogrammed linens and She-Crab Soup (page 148) to Sweet Tea (page 157) and Rainbow Row place cards, transport your party-goers to the cobblestone streets of Charleston with every sip of Meeting Street Punch (page 157) and every bite of Palmetto Praline Pie (page 155).

As a little girl playing in the garden of our Meeting Street house, I often discovered pieces of blue-and-white china. I would quickly gather them up and run to my mother to show her my treasures. Chinese blue-and-white porcelain china was in high demand during the eighteenth and nineteenth centuries and once broken, it was tossed out into the yards. The blue-and-white china was also used as ballast on ships, further explaining why the bits and pieces are found along the coastline and have become a staple on tables all around Charleston.

Of course, I always love sending my friends home with a little "happy," so Rainbow Row sugar cookies are a must.

My tablecloth was created from another visit to the fabric store where I fell in love with the pattern and shades of blue.

 TIP: *Think outside the box with flowers. Miniature boxwoods create a delightful garden feeling to the table and can be doubled as décor after the party.*

Eat

Keep food and drink authentic to the location you're choosing to celebrate. I served traditional Charleston favorites like She-Crab Soup and Benne Wafers (page 152). Guests were served glasses of Sweet Tea (page 157) and Meeting Street Punch (page 157).

She-Crab Soup

1 cup lump crab meat

2 tablespoons butter

1 small onion, grated

3 ribs celery, grated

$\frac{1}{8}$ teaspoon salt

$\frac{1}{8}$ teaspoon pepper

2 cups milk

$\frac{1}{2}$ cup heavy cream

2 tablespoons Worcestershire sauce

2 teaspoons all-purpose flour

1 tablespoon water

4 teaspoons dry sherry

Paprika, for garnish

Place crab in a double boiler and add butter, onion, celery, salt, and pepper. Stir until combined. Add milk, cream, and Worcestershire sauce. Make a paste from flour and water and add to mixture to thicken. Cook over low heat for 30 minutes to 1 hour. Just before serving, add 1 teaspoon of dry sherry to each bowl. Garnish with paprika.

YIELD: 4 SERVINGS

TIP: *Serve mini cornbread muffins alongside the soup course. I served mine in a traditional Charleston sweetgrass basket.*

Charleston Shrimp Salad

- ½ cup mayonnaise
- ½ cup chili sauce
- 1 cup chopped celery
- 2 tablespoons sweet pickle relish
- 1 tablespoon diced pimiento
- 1 tablespoon chopped green pepper
- 1 hard-boiled egg, chopped
- 1 teaspoon mustard
- 1 teaspoon Worcestershire sauce
- ¼ teaspoon red pepper
- 2 pounds medium shrimp, peeled, deveined, and cooked

Mix all the ingredients, except the shrimp, to make the sauce. The shrimp and sauce may be prepared the day before, but keep them separated and refrigerated.

Just before serving, combine the sauce and shrimp and serve in a Parmesan bowl. This tangy sauce is also a wonderful dressing on wedge salads.

YIELD: 8 SERVINGS

Parmesan Bowl

- 12 ounces grated Parmesan cheese

Preheat oven to 375° F.

As a guide, draw eight 3–4-inch circles on a piece of parchment paper.

Fill each circle with cheese. Bake for 5 minutes. Allow to cool for 30 seconds and use a cookie spatula to peel off each Parmesan circle. Quickly press circle over the bottom of a small bowl. Allow to cool and then remove. After they have cooled, place in an airtight container until ready to serve.

YIELD: 8 BOWLS

TIP: *Make smaller 1 to 2-inch circles and leave as flat rounds. These make easy and delicious appetizer bites.*

Benne Wafers

This Lowcountry wafer cookie dates back to colonial times when the sesame ("benne") seeds were brought over from West Africa into the Southern states. With a sweet, nutty taste, the Benne Wafer is a quintessential Charleston treat.

1 cup sesame seeds

$\frac{1}{2}$ cup unsalted butter

2 cups firmly packed brown sugar

1 egg, lightly beaten

1 cup all-purpose flour

$\frac{1}{2}$ teaspoon baking powder

$\frac{1}{2}$ teaspoon salt

1 teaspoon vanilla extract

Preheat oven to 325° F. Toast sesame seeds in a pan until lightly golden and fragrant. Set aside.

With an electric mixer, cream together the butter and sugar. Add in beaten egg and combine until fluffy. In a separate bowl, combine flour with baking powder and salt. Slowly add flour mixture to wet batter. Add in vanilla and sesame seeds.

Drop by the teaspoon onto a parchment-lined baking sheet. Lightly pat down the batter with the back of a greased spoon. Bake for 6–8 minutes, or until lightly golden. Oven times may vary, so watch closely. Allow to cool for 1 minute before removing them from your baking sheet.

YIELD: 96 BENNE WAFERS

Palmetto Praline Pie

1 (9-inch) unbaked deep dish pie crust

2½ cups chopped pecans

1 cup firmly packed brown sugar

1 cup granulated sugar

1 cup heavy whipping cream

1 cup unsalted butter, room temperature

½ teaspoon salt

1 teaspoon vanilla extract

½ cup whole pecans

Preheat oven to 350° F.

Line your pie pan with pie crust. Pierce bottom of dough several times with fork to prevent it from rising. Bake for 15 minutes. Remove from oven and set aside.

In a saucepan, combine chopped pecans, brown sugar, granulated sugar, cream, and butter. Stirring often, cook until temperature reaches 230° F (110° C) on a candy thermometer. Remove from heat and stir in salt and vanilla.

Pour mixture into pie pan and return to oven, reducing temperature to 300° F. Bake for 30 minutes. Remove, decorate top with whole pecans, and allow to cool before refrigerating, at least 2 hours. This helps the pie firm up. Keep refrigerated until ready to serve, either chilled or by warming slices for 5–10 seconds in the microwave before enjoying.

YIELD: 1 (9-INCH) PIE, OR 6-8 SERVINGS

Drink

All Southern hostesses know that sweet tea is non-negotiable. I like to jazz mine up with mint ice cubes served alongside a cocktail as well. You can never go wrong with a fresh mint garnish, and it's quite easy to grow too!

Meeting Street Punch

1 quart Sweet Tea

3 cups peach brandy

¼ cup rum

2 (750 ml) bottles champagne

1 quart sparkling water

Sliced peaches, for garnish

Combine tea, brandy, and rum into a large punch bowl or serving pitcher. Just before serving, stir in champagne and sparkling water. Garnish with peaches.

YIELD: 5 QUARTS

Sweet Tea

2 quarts water

1 cup sugar

4 family size tea bags

Mint ice cubes

Combine water and sugar and bring to a boil. Remove from heat, place the 4 tea bags in the hot water, and let steep for 5 minutes or longer if you want stronger tea. Allow to cool and then refrigerate until very cold, about 4 hours. Serve over ice with mint ice cubes and lemon slices.

YIELD: ½ GALLON

Mint Ice Cubes

Ice cube tray

Water

Mint leaves

Fill ½ of each ice cube square with water. Freeze ice cube tray. Add 1 mint leaf onto each ice cube square and top with water. Freeze and enjoy.

TIP: *If time is of the essence, place the mint leaf at the bottom of the cube and fill with water before freezing. The double freeze simply places the mint leaf in the middle of the ice cube for the prettiest presentation.*

Día de los Muertos Fiesta

"To invite a person to your house is to take charge of his happiness as long as he is beneath your roof." —Brillat-Savarin

Día de los Muertos (Day of the Dead) is a multi-day Mexican holiday focused on celebrating the lives and spiritual journeys of family and friends who have passed away. From building *ofrendas* (altars, or "offerings") to honoring the dead with sugar skulls and festive parades, there are a number of unique and celebratory traditions you can incorporate into a Día de los Muertos Fiesta.

Honor loved ones who have passed away by incorporating photographs and memorabilia throughout the party.

Serve up colorful skull sugar cookies as a sweet treat or as a take-home favor for guests. You can also recreate the idea with mini cakes as well.

Succulents tucked down in colorful containers provide both a fabulous favor for guests as well as décor for the tablescape. Similarly, a large cactus makes the perfect centerpiece for the table.

A simple wooden table is given an instant boost of color with a serape table runner in vibrant colors. You can use any similar Mexican-style blanket or throw as a table runner.

In addition to the Day of the Dead, you can also pull inspirational elements for Cinco de Mayo festivities from this party as well.

Eat

Serve foods that are easy to eat, like mini tacos and empanadas. My mini taco tip is a personal favorite and countless friends have thanked me for this easy idea, especially when serving tacos to children. You can fill it with your favorite ingredients or follow my ground beef Mini Taco recipe below.

Mini Tacos

5 soft flour tortillas

1 pound ground beef

1 medium onion, chopped

1 teaspoon chili powder

$\frac{1}{2}$ teaspoon garlic powder

$\frac{1}{2}$ teaspoon salt

$\frac{1}{2}$ cup Cotija cheese, crumbled

$\frac{1}{2}$ cup diced tomatoes

Fresh cilantro, for garnish

Preheat oven to 350° F.

Use a round cookie cutter (I used a 3-inch round cutter) to cut out as many mini taco shells as you want from the flour tortillas. Lightly spray with cooking spray and microwave for 10 seconds to make pliable. Turn a muffin tin upside down and spray with nonstick cooking spray. Place your warm taco shells (folded in half) between the muffin spaces so they will bake in a "taco" shape. Bake for 5–7 minutes, or until lightly golden.

In a medium nonstick skillet, brown ground beef and onion for 8–10 minutes, or until beef is cooked thoroughly. Drain and stir in chili powder, garlic powder, and salt. Keep warm on simmer until ready to assemble tacos.

Fill each baked mini taco with ground beef, crumbled Cotija, diced tomatoes, and garnish with diced cilantro.

YIELD: 20 MINI TACOS

TIP: *Lean mini tacos against lime wedges as a helpful way to keep them upright. Guests can then add a squeeze of the lime to their tacos before enjoying.*

Pan de Muertos

Spanish for "bread of the dead," this Mexican favorite is traditionally baked in the days and weeks leading up to Día de los Muertos. Bone shapes are often added to the top of the sweet bread. I made smaller versions of this bread for easier eating.

3/4 cup granulated sugar, divided

1/2 teaspoon salt

1 teaspoon anise seeds

2 (1/4-ounce) packets active dry yeast

1/2 cup whole milk

1/2 cup water

1/2 cup (1 stick) unsalted butter

4 large eggs

5 1/2–6 cups all-purpose flour

1/4 cup orange juice

2 teaspoons orange zest

Powdered sugar, for dusting

In a small mixing bowl, combine 1/2 cup sugar, salt, anise seeds, and yeast. Stir to combine. In a saucepan over medium heat, combine milk, water, and butter. Once butter has melted, add it to the yeast mixture and mix to combine. Add in eggs and 1 1/2 cups of flour. Beat well with electric mixer. Add in 4 cups flour, 1/2 cup at a time.

Turn out dough on a floured surface and knead for 10 minutes, or until dough is smooth, elastic, and no longer sticky. Knead in additional 1/2 cup flour if needed. Place in a lightly oiled bowl and cover with plastic wrap. In a warm space, allow to rise for 1 1/2 hours, or until doubled in size.

Punch dough down in middle and divide into 4 to 6 small balls. Pinch off a piece of dough from each ball to make skull shapes. Lay the skull shapes across the top of the balls. Set aside on baking sheet to rise for 1 additional hour.

Preheat oven to 350° F.

In a saucepan, combine orange juice, remaining 1/4 cup sugar, and orange zest. Heat until boiling and brush over top of dough before baking. Bake for 20–25 minutes, until golden, or longer if making larger rolls. Dust with powdered sugar before serving.

 TIP: *Marigolds are a flower traditionally used during Día de los Muertos festivities: use them as centerpiece décor or simply as a touch of color on a serving platter or cake stand.*

YIELD: 2 LARGE PAN DE MUERTOS, OR 6 MINI PAN DE MUERTOS

Drink

Set up a party bar with authentic Mexican sodas like Jarritos. The colors of the bottles are vivid, and they taste delicious as well! For another delicious beverage, serve Mini Champurrados, a thick Mexican hot chocolate, which makes the perfect finish to your Día de los Muertos dinner. Look for mini drink containers at party stores (see Resources on page 194) for the perfect mini size. I especially love this idea for very sweet drinks when guests might just want a little taste.

Mini Champurrados

- **3 cups water**
- **2 cinnamon sticks**
- **1 (3-ounce) tablet Mexican chocolate (found in the international aisle)**
- **½ cup firmly packed brown sugar**
- **2½ cups whole milk**
- **¼ cup masa corn flour**

In a medium saucepan, combine water and cinnamon sticks. Heat over medium heat until boiling. Add in chocolate and stir until melted. Stir in brown sugar.

In a separate bowl, combine milk and masa corn flour until thick and smooth without lumps. Whisk the masa flour mixture into the chocolate and stir quickly to combine. Allow to cook and thicken for 10 minutes, stirring occasionally. Remove cinnamon sticks and serve.

YIELD: 6 FULL-SIZE SERVINGS, OR 18 MINI SERVINGS

Grapefruit Margaritas

- **4 cups ruby red grapefruit juice**
- **2 cups agave tequila**
- **1 cup agave syrup**
- **1 fresh lime, squeezed**

Combine juice, tequila, and syrup until thoroughly mixed. Squeeze in lime juice and stir. Pour over ice in margarita glasses, or serve in unique mini skull glasses for a Día de los Muertos toast.

 TIP: *Visit your liquor store to find unique miniature bottles that are often perfect additions to your parties, like these mini skulls I filled with grapefruit margaritas.*

YIELD: 6 MARGARITAS, OR 12 MINI MARGARITAS

Black and White Masquerade Party

"Serve the dinner backward, do anything—but for goodness sake, do something weird." —Elsa Maxwell

Follow in the footsteps of Truman Capote and host the ultimate party; a Black and White Masquerade Party! While your event doesn't have to include formal dancing or hundreds of guests, you can easily host a classy dinner party with all the same decorative touches.

Find inspiration from this dinner party for countless occasions from birthday dinners to engagement parties. My own wedding was a black-and-white striped affair. Encourage your guests to wear black and white by including it as a note on the invitation.

To recreate the look, top your table with a solid black tablecloth and a black-and-white striped runner. These are both tablecloths I highly recommend keeping on hand as you will find lots of uses for them year-round (black for Halloween, striped runner for football parties, birthdays, etc.).

Pull out all your candelabras and candle holders to create a glowing ambiance.

TIP: *I love to add instax cameras to my party tables, especially at costume parties. Guests can snap away and have photos to take home as a memento!*

What truly sets this party apart are the balloons. You can keep balloons elegant by sticking only to black and white (with coordinating ribbons) and letting them fill your party room by the dozens. For a more playful twist on this idea, use multicolored balloons for a child's party. Guests old and young love this festive touch.

Top each place setting with a mask for every guest. They make for fabulous photo props and a fun favor for your guests to take home.

Eat

Mix and match your favorite recipes from the ones found in this party as well as others throughout the book. I love the Beet and Cheese Layered Salad because the bright red really pops against the black and white. The Red Velvet Brownie Truffle Cakes are Pizzazzerie's most popular recipe over the last seven years, so I knew I had to include it for you here. It's a must-try!

Beet and Cheese Layered Salad

3 red beets

4 ounces goat cheese

Chopped fresh chives, for garnish

Parsley sprigs, for garnish

Preheat the oven to 350° F.

Rinse beets and brush with olive oil. Wrap aluminum foil around each beet and bake on baking sheet for 60–70 minutes, or until a fork enters the center easily. Allow to cool and peel skin off beets. Slice into $\frac{1}{4}$-inch slices. Use a small cookie cutter ($1\frac{1}{2}$ to 2-inch) to cut out circles from the beets. Set aside.

Slice goat cheese into $\frac{1}{4}$-inch slices, and then cut out circles with cutter. Carefully stack the beet and cheese circles in layers. Garnish with chives and a sprig of parsley.

YIELD: 6 LAYERED SALADS

 TIP: *To jazz up simple appetizers and mini salads, serve them atop a small basil or lettuce leaf.*

Easy White Chocolate Mousse

12 ounces white chocolate, chopped

1 pint whipping cream

¼ teaspoon salt

1 teaspoon vanilla extract

Using a double boiler, melt white chocolate until smooth. Pour whipping cream into an electric mixer bowl. Whisk on high until soft peaks form. Add salt and vanilla until combined. Slowly fold in melted white chocolate. Refrigerate until ready to serve. Spoon or pipe into containers.

YIELD: 6-8 MINI DESSERTS

Red Velvet Brownie Truffle Cakes

1 (16.5-ounce) box red velvet cake mix

½ cup butter, melted

2 eggs

1 (3.3-ounce) package Jell-O instant white chocolate or vanilla-flavored pudding

6 tablespoons vegetable oil

1 (14.3-ounce) package Oreos

8 ounces cream cheese

1½ cups semisweet chocolate chips

½ cup mini chocolate chips, for garnish

Preheat oven to 325° F.

Combine cake mix, butter, eggs, pudding mix, and vegetable oil in a large mixing bowl. Beat with electric mixer until thoroughly combined. Spray a 9 x 13-inch baking pan with nonstick cooking spray. Spread the batter into the pan, all the way to the edges. Batter is very thick. Bake for 20–22 minutes, or until a toothpick inserted into the center comes out clean (ovens vary so watch closely). Allow to cool.

Use a food processor to crush Oreos until smooth. Melt cream cheese for 15 seconds in a microwave to soften. Stir together crushed Oreos and cream cheese until combined. Carefully spread out Oreo truffle mixture on top of baked red velvet brownies. Melt semisweet chocolate and pour over top Oreo truffle layer. Sprinkle with mini chocolate chips while still warm. Allow to cool, and then cut with a circle cookie cutter or biscuit cutter.

YIELD: 10 ROUND CAKES, OR 12 SQUARES

Drink

Find mini black-and-white martini glasses at party stores (often found with other appetizer dishes) and use them for appetizers and mini cocktails to greet guests with upon arrival. Fill each mini cocktail with a mini bow tie drink stirrer for an extra touch of whimsy!

White Chocolate Martini

- **1 ounce vanilla vodka**
- **1.5 ounces white chocolate liqueur**
- **2 ounces heavy cream**

Combine vanilla vodka, white chocolate liqueur, and heavy cream. Keep chilled until ready to serve.

YIELD: 1 COCKTAIL

A Christmas Dinner

"Christmas waves a magic wand over this world and behold, everything is softer and more beautiful." —Norman Vincent Peale

One simply cannot share a year of entertaining ideas without touching on the most magical holiday of all—Christmas! Entertaining during the holidays has a little extra sparkle about it whether it's a dinner party, caroling parties, hot cocoa parties, or a cookie-decorating event for the little ones. No matter what size or style, your party helps make time to be with the people you love.

One of my favorite style icons is Kate Spade, and what better way to incorporate traditional Kate Spade elements than for a party during the most magical time of the year?

I began with a Kate Spade–inspired color combo: aqua and green. Using it throughout the tablescape, I topped a green tablecloth with an ornament garland table runner made with aqua and green baubles. You can easily recreate this idea in your own favorite color scheme. See "DIY Ornament Table Runner" on page 191 for how-to instructions.

Sprigs of rosemary in the champagne flutes and whimsical patterned desserts help add those party details that I just love.

One of my favorite details was a nod to one of Kate Spade's signature design elements, a party bow! Using two colored pieces of ribbon, we tied the flatware together to top each plate.

Guests also had their very own mini nutcracker in the party colors. You can find wooden nutcrackers in all sizes from craft stores and easily spray paint them to fit your color scheme.

TIP: *If you can't find the perfect plates for your color scheme, add a charger that's been spray painted in the party hues underneath the dinner plate (see page 33 for how-to instructions).*

Eat

Holiday parties are the time to bring out your favorite tried-and-true recipes. The ones I chose for this holiday party are both easy and delicious. You can customize the canapé idea with your own favorite filling or go with my crab recipe below. Love the polka dots on the dessert but want to incorporate them in a different way? Top brownie squares or a large round cake with a festive pattern for a showstopping dessert.

Crab Canapés

2 (6-ounce) cans lump crab meat, drained

$1^1/_2$ cups finely grated cheddar cheese

$^1/_4$ cup mayonnaise

2 green onions, chopped

2 tablespoons horseradish

1 teaspoon lemon juice

$^1/_2$ teaspoon pepper

40 phyllo cups

Preheat oven to 325° F.

Combine all the ingredients and mix well. Refrigerate until needed. Spoon into phyllo cups and bake on baking sheet for 8–10 minutes, or until cheese melts.

YIELD: 40 CANAPÉS

Gingerbread Cake Parfaits

⅓ cup butter, melted

⅓ cup firmly packed light brown sugar

⅓ cup sugar

½ cup molasses

2 eggs, room temperature

½ cup milk

1 (8-ounce) container sour cream

1¾ cups all-purpose flour

1 teaspoon baking soda

¼ teaspoon salt

2 teaspoons cinnamon

¼ teaspoon nutmeg

1 teaspoon ground ginger

½ teaspoon ground cloves

CREAM CHEESE FROSTING

8 ounces cream cheese, room temperature

½ cup butter, softened

1 teaspoon vanilla extract

1 (1-pound) package powdered sugar

GINGERBREAD CAKE

Preheat oven to 350° F.

Mix together the butter, sugars, molasses, eggs, milk, and sour cream. In a separate mixing bowl, stir together flour, baking soda, salt, cinnamon, nutmeg, ginger, and cloves. Gradually add dry ingredients to wet ingredients, mixing well. Bake for 20 minutes in a 9 x 13-inch baking pan sprayed with nonstick cooking spray. Cool slightly and cut into 8 circles (roughly 2½ to 3 inches). Lay each circle on its side and slice into two circles. You can also cut cake into squares or other shapes to fit your serving dish.

CREAM CHEESE FROSTING

Beat cream cheese, butter, and vanilla with an electric mixer until well blended. Add powdered sugar, 1 cup at a time, and continue to blend well.

ASSEMBLY

Layer cake rounds with frosting in between. On top of cake, lay down a patterned stencil (from craft store or simply use a hole punch on card stock) and dust with powdered sugar. Carefully lift off the stencil to reveal a beautiful design! You could also use this idea to spell out names or letters for birthdays or other special occasions.

YIELD: 8 PARFAITS

Sugared Holly Leaves

Holly leaves

Egg whites

Granulated sugar

Dip holly leaves into egg whites. Next, dip the coated leaves into a bowl of granulated sugar. Shake the excess sugar off and place on a piece of parchment paper to dry. These leaves can be prepared several days in advance. They add a special touch to any dessert or serving platter during the holidays.

Drink

Holiday parties are the ultimate time to pop the champagne! I love mixed cocktails, but every hostess needs a simple champagne cocktail that's ready in mere seconds (leaving more time to get dressed and ready for the party!). The rosemary sprig lends a perfect festive touch your guests will love.

Rosemary Champagne Cocktail

1 cup St-Germain, chilled

1 (750 ml) bottle champagne, chilled

Rosemary sprigs

Fill each glass with 1 ounce St-Germain. Top with 5 ounces champagne, and stir with a rosemary sprig.

YIELD: 5 COCKTAILS

Create

Mini Party Table

Since my daughter was born several years ago, she has naturally found herself looking on as my mother and I style tablescapes on a daily basis. Blakely has quickly fallen in love with the art of setting her own party tables for her teddy bears.

My mother had a small wooden table and chairs made that we set beside our own table while we work. We always hand Blakely a few napkins and little plates to "work" alongside us. Her teddy bear parties are quite the occasion, and you can find me sharing them often on Instagram and Pizzazzerie.com under #blakelystables. While working on this Christmas design, Blakely took a particular liking to the party, so we helped her create a miniature replica of the larger table. Here are a few tips (opposite page) if you'd like to create a child's version of your adult party table.

- *Buy a small piece of coordinating fabric to create a tablecloth, or cut down an extra tablecloth to match.*

- *Use small appetizer plates as the children's dinner plates.*

- *Try sherry glasses as "champagne glasses" (to be filled with apple juice, of course). You can also find mini plastic glasses at party stores.*

- *Cut down paper straws and cocktail napkins with scissors to make them "child size."*

- *Perfect your mini place settings with demitasse spoons or appetizer forks.*

DIY Ornament Table Runner

Ribbon

Ornament baubles

Scissors

Measure your ribbon to match the length of your table and allow for overhang if you wish the table runner to extend down the ends of the table. Gather ornaments in different sizes, textures, and colors to complement your table décor. Thread the ornament hooks onto the ribbon, alternating size, texture, and color. Once your table runner has reached the desired length, tie a knot at the end of the ribbon at both ends to secure the ornaments. Carefully drape across the center of your table.

RECERPE INDEX

Appetizers

Breads

Cakes

Cookies and Bars

Desserts

Drinks

Salads

Sandwiches & Soups

Treats

Metric Conversion Chart

Volume Measurements		Weight Measurements		Temperature Conversion	
U.S.	*Metric*	*U.S.*	*Metric*	*Fahrenheit*	*Celsius*
1 teaspoon	5 ml	½ ounce	15 g	250	120
1 tablespoon	15 ml	1 ounce	30 g	300	150
¼ cup	60 ml	3 ounces	90 g	325	160
⅓ cup	75 ml	4 ounces	115 g	350	180
½ cup	125 ml	8 ounces	225 g	375	190
⅔ cup	150 ml	12 ounces	350 g	400	200
¾ cup	175 ml	1 pound	450 g	425	220
1 cup	250 ml	2¼ pounds	1 kg	450	230

RESOURCES

New Year's Day Brunch

Glitter tablecloth: Amazon (amazon.com)

Bar cart: Grandin Road (grandinroad.com)

Dinnerware and flatware: Olivia & Oliver (bedbathandbeyond.com)

Champagne flutes: Waterford Crystal

Mini vases: Michaels (michaels.com)

Mini confetti boxes: Paper Mart (papermart.com)

Cheers tags: Kate Spade (katespade.com)

Mini pink cake stand: Mosser Glass (mosserglass.com)

Gold foil sheets: Michaels (michaels.com)

Cake stands: HomeGoods (homegoods.com)

Derby Party

Small silver ice bucket: Draper James (draperjames.com)

Julep cups: Julep Cups (julepcups.com)

Horseshoe stir sticks: Pick On Us (pickonus.com)

Green striped fabric: Jo-Ann Fabric and Craft Stores (joann.com)

Mini silver trophies: Party City (partycity.com)

Mini wooden picket fence: Michaels (michaels.com)

A Birthday Celebration for Her

Tablecloth and napkins: Lacefield Designs (lacefielddesigns.com)

Wooden name calligraphy: Hardink Calligraphy (hardinkcalligraphy.com)

Lasercut Wooden Names: Kolorize (etsy.com/shop/kolorize)

Dinnerware, flatware, and cocktail glasses: Olivia & Oliver (bedbathandbeyond.com)

Party hats: Oh Joy! for Target (target.com)

Cake stand: HomeGoods (homegoods.com)

A Modern May Day Lunch

High back chairs: Carleton Varney for Frontgate (frontgate.com)

Lunch baskets: Cost Plus World Market (worldmarket.com)

Pink cake stand: Mosser Glass (mosserglass.com)

Pink glasses: vintage

Craft flowers: Michaels (michaels.com)

Sip Sip Hooray napkins: Slant Collections (slantcollections.com)

White square tray: West Elm (westelm.com)

Wedding Anniversary Party

Silver garland backdrop: Amazon (amazon.com)

Mini silver letters and large "25" numbers: Michaels (michaels.com)

Spoon cookie cutter: The Cookie Cutter Shop (etsy.com/shop/TheCookieCutterShop)

Edible silver leaf: Amazon (amazon.com)

Silver fabric: Jo-Ann Fabric and Craft Stores (joann.com)

Bastille Day Fête

Plates: HomeGoods (homegoods.com)

Tablecloth fabric: Nate Berkus Fabrics (joann.com)

Champagne flutes: Kate Spade (katespade.com)

Eiffel tower: Homegoods (homegoods.com)

French lemonade: Cost Plus World Market (worldmarket.com)

Red flatware: Homegoods (homegoods.com)

Mini French flags: Amazon (amazon.com)

Book Club Gathering

Miniature wooden boards: Webstaurant Store (webstaurantstore.com)

Library card menus and book cover place mats: Harper Gray (harpergray.net)

Wooden cutlery: Harlow & Grey (harlowandgrey.com)

Cheers stir sticks: Erin Haines Design Co. (etsy.com/shop/ErinHainesDesignCo)

Wooden craft letters: Michaels (michaels.com)

Calligraphy book marks: Kerith Stanton

A Dapper Birthday Celebration for Him

Dapper stir sticks: 43Layers (43layers.com)

Wooden chargers: Rustic Wood Slices (etsy.com/shop/RusticWoodSlices)

Liquor bottle cakes: Faboo Cakes (faboocakes.com)

Venue: Bloomsbury Farms (bloomsburyfarms.com)

Wooden cutlery: Shop Sweet Lulu (shopsweetlulu.com)

Autumnal Equinox Party

Invitation and food labels: WH Hostess Social Stationery (whhostess.com)

Monogrammed napkins: LBOriginals (etsy.com/shop/preppypapergirl)

Pillows: Minted (minted.com)

Rose gold flatware: Olivia & Oliver (bedbathandbeyond.com)

White dinnerware: Pier 1 Imports (pier1.com)

Copper martini glasses: Pier 1 Imports (pier1.com)

Charleston Garden Party

Monogram linens: Halo Home by KSW (halohomebyksw.com)

Tablecloth: Lacefield Designs (lacefielddesigns.com)

Custom painted Rainbow Row place cards: Kori Clark (koriclark.com)

Single house cookies: The Baked Equation (thebakedequation.com)

Mini ice bucket: Draper James (draperjames.com)

Día de los Muertos Fiesta

Mini skull glasses: Crystal Head Vodka (crystalheadvodka.com)

Sugar skull cookies: The Baked Equation (thebakedequation.com)

Table runner, napkins, tissue banners: MexFabric Supplies (mexfabricsupplies.com)

Party printables: Lindi Haws (love-the-day.com)

Gold flatware: Unison (unisonhome.com)

Clear mini mugs: Party City (partycity.com)

Gold straws: Shop Sweet Lulu (shopsweetlulu.com)

Black and White Masquerade Party

Masks: Craft stores; Amazon (amazon.com)

Black-and-white striped fabric: Jo-Ann Fabric and Craft Stores (joann.com)

Gold candelabras: Lights & Décor (lightsforalloccasions.com)

Black-and-white striped salad plate: Ralph Lauren at Homegoods (homegoods.com)

Mini black-and-white martini glasses: Party City (partycity.com)

A Christmas Dinner

Blue-rimmed plates: Kate Spade (katespade.com)

Champagne flutes: Kate Spade (katespade.com)

Green tablecloth: Kate Spade (katespade.com)

Mini wooden nutcrackers: Jo-Ann Fabric and Craft Stores (joann.com)

Ornaments: Hobby Lobby (hobbylobby.com)

MIX IT UP

While you'll find over a dozen celebratory occasions detailed in this book, I simply didn't have the space to include them all. No worries! There are hundreds of combinations within the pages of this book to pull together all kinds of gatherings. Here are a few of my favorites . . .

Bridal Shower

Celebrate the bride-to-be with a chic affair! From blush pink to floral hues, recreate the New Year's Day Brunch (page 21) with mini framed childhood photos of the bridesmaids as place cards.

Baby Shower

Serve up a spring-themed shower with tips from the Modern May Day Lunch (page 65). Or combine elements of the Book Club Gathering (page 105) with the Dapper Birthday Celebration (page 119) for a rustic, nature-themed shower for the mom-to-be.

Kid's Party

Serve up mini versions of favorite kid foods like Mini Tacos (page 162) and Mini Cheddar Biscuits (page 108). Opt for multicolored balloons to fill the room as seen in the Black and White Masquerade Party (page 171).

Valentine's Day

This holiday deserves lots of love as well! Mini Rose Cakes (page 71) served alongside Pink Lemonade Punch Cocktails (page 61) combine for the perfect Valentine's Day duo!

Easter

Gather Easter inspiration from the Modern May Day Lunch (page 65) and add brightly colored eggs down the center of the table, or top them on a long charcuterie board similar to the one in the Book Club Gathering (page 105).

Cinco de Mayo

One of my favorite days of the year. Gather inspiration from the Día de los Muertos Fiesta (page 159). Cheers to the occasion with Grapefruit Margaritas (page 168) and Mini Tacos (page 162).

Graduation

Celebrating a momentous graduation? Create a photo backdrop similar to the silver one in the Wedding Anniversary Party (page 79) for all those memorable snapshots! Top a cake with flowers in the school colors for a sweet touch.

Backyard Barbecues

The perfect way to celebrate warmer weather! I suggest serving up Sriracha and Bourbon Wings (page 127) and finishing the night with Bacon and Pecan S'mores (page 124). This is also the perfect opportunity to utilize the DIY Low Dining Table (page 142).

Fourth of July

Gather inspiration from the red, white, and blue festivities of the Bastille Day Fête (page 91).

Going-Away Party

Moving away can be a bittersweet occasion. Make it festive by adding touches of city tributes to the table like in the Charleston Garden Party (page 145). Serve up iconic foods (such as hot chicken for a Nashville-themed party or pizza by the slice for a New York–themed party).

Halloween

Set the stage for a spooky yet chic Halloween party from the Black and White Masquerade Party (page 171). Supply masks for the guests, serve appetizers in carved out pumpkins (page 136), and hand out drinks in mini skull glasses (page 168).

Thanksgiving

Set a gorgeous Thanksgiving table with fall leaves and rustic touches from the Autumnal Equinox Party (page 133). In addition to the Caramel Apple Martini (page 141), the Spicy Maple Bourbon Cocktail (page 131) would be a fabulous addition to Thanksgiving dinner.

Dessert Party

Pull a few of your favorites to combine for a very delicious occasion. I suggest the Bacon and Pecan S'mores (page 124), Red Velvet Brownie Truffle Cakes (page 176), and Palmetto Praline Pie (page 155).

Birthdays

Serve up the Crêpe Cake (page 101) for a nontraditional birthday cake. Just add candles and sprinkles for the finishing touch.

New Year's Eve

While there's a whole chapter dedicated to throwing a glitzy New Year's Day Brunch, here are some ideas to get you started on planning a fabulous New Year's Eve party. Incorporate mini champagne bottles (page 80), balloon décor (page 173), DIY Custom Party Horns (page 62), and the Rosemary Champagne Cocktail (page 189) to create a custom countdown celebration.

ACKNOWLEDGMENTS

I'd like to thank each and every person who helped make this book possible. To my editor Katie Killebrew, for allowing me the opportunity to bring this dream to life; thank you for your guidance and ceaseless efforts. To my mother, for quite literally being my right hand gal day in and day out to create this book; I could not have done it without you. Thank you to Evin Krehbiel for bringing these pages to life through your gorgeous photography, and for being a constant cheerleader from start to finish. Thank you to my family (Chris, Blakely, and George, too) for supporting me and being by my side while I worked on this book. Thank you also for allowing me to turn our house into a daily party for an entire year!

Special thanks to Mandy Reeves, Erica Braden, Jessica Hsu, Ashley Seth, Elizabeth Downing, Jana Fowler, Autumn McEntire Sizemore, Luke Krehbiel, Arjun Seth, Rinne Sade, Kimberly Schlegel Whitman, Ruth Smith, Tami Polak, Natalie Benz, Melissa Barbakoff, Lindi Haws, Jill Rigsby, Rebecca June Smith, Sean and Bethany Rogers, Allie Miller, Elizabeth Hardin, Laurie Byrne, Kelly Lyden, David Dial, David Dial Jr., Laura Dial, and Robbie Dial for all of your help both big and small.

Growing up in the South, **COURTNEY WHITMORE** has always loved the art of presenting classic Southern foods with a modern twist and setting a tablescape with lots of pizzazz. She attended Vanderbilt University earning both a bachelors in communications and a masters in organizational leadership. In 2010, she left her full-time job as a career counselor to launch Pizzazzerie.com (pronounced piz·zazze·rie [pəˈzaz ərē]) to share entertaining inspiration and ideas with readers around the world.

When she's not working on her next book, Courtney styles and creates content for a variety of publications and brands such as HGTV, *Better Homes & Gardens,* Target, Coca-Cola, Lindt Chocolate, Yoplait, Pepperidge Farm, Frontgate, and more to connect consumers with their products in an entertaining setting. She is also the author of three cookbooks: *Push-Up Pops, Candy Making for Kids,* and *Frostings.*

She lives in Nashville, Tennessee, with her husband, daughter (commonly referred to as #babypizzazzerie), and Irish Setter (George).

PHRONSIE DIAL is a creative stylist and tablescape designer who works on brand partnerships and special projects for Pizzazzerie.com. Over the past two decades, she has created countless DIY party ideas and crafts for magazines and news outlets. She loves to throw parties that create lifelong memories and also happens to be one-half of this mother/daughter duo as Courtney's mom.

EVIN KREHBIEL is the creative talent and energetic personality behind Evin Photography. Since 2005, Evin Photography has established itself as a highly sought-after photography company in Nashville, Tennessee, and throughout the South. Evin is an ambitious entrepreneur as well as a loving wife to Luke, and mom to three beautiful children, Cohen, Kinzie, and Leyton.

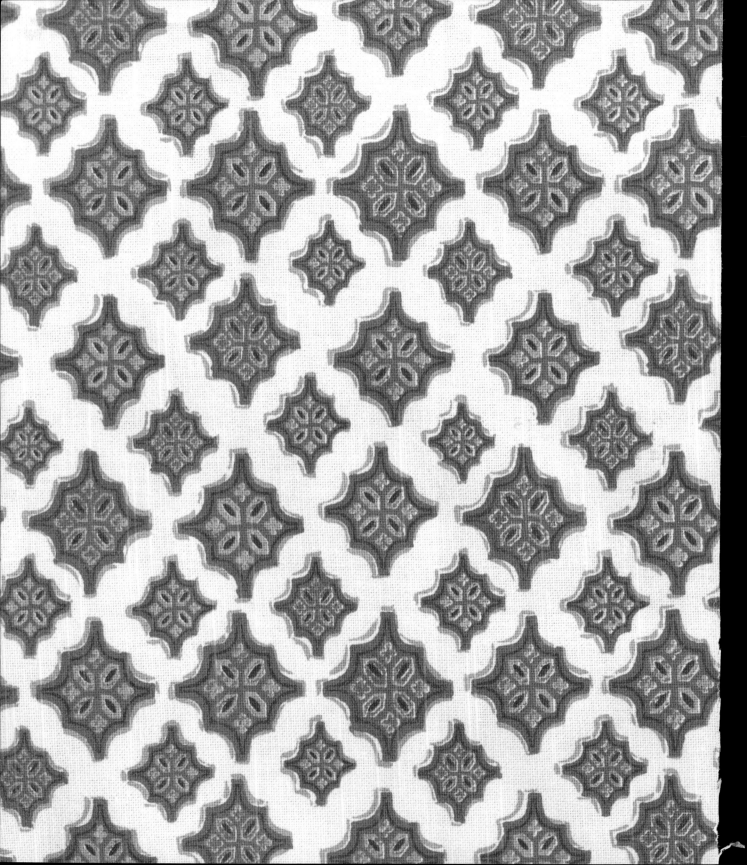